My desire for every Lenten season is to come out of it spiritually stronger. I am greatly encouraged as I share with you this new work, *Ashes To Alleluia,* by Bishop Sharma D. Lewis Logan and Dr. Lewis Logan. This husband and wife duo have penned a meditation volume that is guaranteed to inspire, inform, and ignite fresh fire and insights for those who will read it!

Bishop John R. Bryant
Retired, African Methodist Episcopal Church

ASHES TO ALLELUIA

40 Days to Transformational Discipleship

**BISHOP SHARMA D. LEWIS LOGAN
DR. LEWIS E. LOGAN, II**

Ashes to Alleluia
40 Days to Transformational Discipleship

by Bishop Sharma D. Lewis Logan & Dr. Lewis E. Logan, II

©2025 Market Square Publishing
books@marketsquarebooks.com
141 N. Martinwood, Suite 2 Knoxville, Tennessee 37923

ISBN: 978-1-950899-97-5

Printed and Bound in the United States of America
Cover Illustration & Book Design ©2025 Market Square Publishing, LLC

Editor: Sheri Carder Hood
Cover Design: Kevin Slimp
Page Design: Ashley Burton

All rights reserved. No part of this book may be reproduced in any manner without written permission except in the case of brief quotations included in critical articles and reviews. For information, please contact Market Square Publishing, LLC.

Scripture quotations used with permission from:

NRSVue
The New Revised Standard Version Updated Edition.
Copyright © 2021 National Council of Churches of Christ in the United States of America.
Used by permission. All rights reserved worldwide.

NIV
Scriptures marked NIV are taken from the NEW INTERNATIONAL VERSION (NIV): Scripture taken from THE HOLY BIBLE, NEW INTERNATIONAL VERSION ®. Copyright© 1973, 1978, 1984, 2011 by Biblica, Inc.™. Used by permission of Zondervan.

NLT
Scriptures marked NLT are taken from the HOLY BIBLE, NEW LIVING TRANSLATION (NLT): Scriptures taken from the HOLY BIBLE, NEW LIVING TRANSLATION, Copyright© 1996, 2004, 2007 by Tyndale House Foundation. Used by permission of Tyndale House Publishers, Inc., Carol Stream, Illinois 60188. All rights reserved. Used by permission.

NKJV
Scriptures marked NKJV are taken from the NEW KING JAMES VERSION (NKJV): Scripture taken from the NEW KING JAMES VERSION®. Copyright© 1982 by Thomas Nelson, Inc. Used by permission. All rights reserved.

CEB
Scripture quotations from the COMMON ENGLISH BIBLE. © Copyright 2011 COMMON ENGLISH BIBLE. All rights reserved. Used by permission.

Contents

Introduction 1
Our Authors Lead Us Into the Lenten Season

Ash Wednesday 5
Drop the Mic

First Thursday of Lent 9
Forgiveness

First Friday of Lent 13
Confessions of a Prophetic Hitman

First Saturday of Lent 19
The Childlike Faith

First Monday of Lent 23
He is Like Us

First Tuesday of Lent 27
Forgiveness

Second Wednesday of Lent 31
From Refusal to Release

Second Thursday of Lent 35
My Help

Second Friday of Lent 39
Awesome!

Second Saturday of Lent 43
The Gentiles' Faith

Second Monday of Lent 47
"SMH" (Shaking My Head)

Second Tuesday of Lent 51
Facing Death

Third Wednesday of Lent 55
The Ultimate Finisher

Third Thursday of Lent 59
Worship

Third Friday of Lent 63
The Gift of Good Company

Third Saturday of Lent 67
A Divine Encounter

Third Monday of Lent 71
"Way Maker"

Third Tuesday of Lent 75
Obedience

Fourth Wednesday of Lent 79
Spoiler Alert

Fourth Thursday of Lent 83
Words
Fourth Friday of Lent 87
Don't Act Your Age
Fourth Saturday of Lent 91
The Shepherd
Fourth Monday of Lent 95
Transformational Experiences
Fourth Tuesday of Lent 99
"Praise Is What I Do!"
Fifth Wednesday of Lent 103
Title: Isness and Oughtness
Fifth Thursday of Lent 107
The Angel and the Scroll
Fifth Friday of Lent 111
Focused!
Fifth Saturday of Lent 115
Hope in the Midst of Hardship
Fifth Monday of Lent 119
Shut Up by Shame
Fifth Tuesday of Lent 123
Save Me
Sixth Wednesday of Lent 127
Cardiac Bypass
Sixth Thursday of Lent 131
When Believers Pray ...
Sixth Friday of Lent 135
The Struggle Is Real
Sixth Saturday of Lent 139
Death
Sixth Monday of Lent 143
Preparation Meets Opportunity
Sixth Tuesday of Lent 147
Aged and In Trouble
Betrayal Wednesday 151
Inside Job
Maundy Thursday 155
L-O-V-E
Good Friday 159
Bring it!
Holy Saturday 163
What Will People Remember?
Group Study Guides 165

INTRODUCTION

Our Authors Lead Us Into the Lenten Season

Bishop Sharma D. Lewis Logan

Lent has always been one of my favorite seasons during the Christian year. As a believer, it allows me to set aside concentrated time for introspection, renewal, prayer, fasting, and reading of God's Word. I wrote these devotionals through the lens of both a child and an older adult, celebrating the power of Jesus Christ's life, death, and resurrection. My prayer is that individuals and groups will experience spiritual nourishment and enrichment as they walk through the forty days of this Lenten study.

Dr. Lewis E. Logan, II

The Lenten Journey: Preparation and Challenge

Just as Jesus emerged from forty days of preparation led by the Holy Spirit, we, too, are readied to confront our own era's challenges with wisdom and courage rooted in the Word. This time, beginning at the Jordan and marked by intensive trial, is a precursor for the ongoing experience of discipleship on our spiritual journey.

Facing Modern Pressures

Viewing Lent as a temporary inconvenience risks overlooking three persistent and profound pressures—internal and external—which shape our lives in this postmodern world. Like Jesus, who endured the hardships of a lowly tekton (craftsman) under oppressive Roman rule and labored among massive state-sanctioned projects near Nazareth, we also live amidst violence, war, and economic upheaval.

Parallels to Jesus' Context

We find ourselves in societies marked by unprecedented wealth and power, yet we witness the consequences of immense disparities daily. The divide between those who have and those who lack not only dehumanizes but fragments communities. Jesus' wilderness experience during Lent becomes our essential process and the "cost of discipleship," as theologian Dietrich Bonhoeffer would say, calling us to embody God's enduring presence in the present, even as we await fulfillment in the imminent future.

Applying Ancient Wisdom in Modern Times

The Lenten Season devotion offers a daily opportunity to apply ancient texts to contemporary existential complexities. The Apostle John drew from the "fall of humanity" narrative in Genesis 3 when warning in 1 John 2:16 (NLT) that "the world offers only craving for physical pleasure, a craving for everything we see, and pride in our achievements and possessions."

Similarly, Dr. Martin Luther King Jr.'s description of the "giant triplets" of racism, materialism, and militarism as ongoing obstacles to justice and peace is as relevant today as it was in 1967. In the forty days ahead, if the same Holy Spirit is leading us that led Jesus, the Apostle Paul, the Apostle John, and Dr. King, then we should expect to learn by encountering similar challenges. Through this forty-day journey together, we are invited to grapple with these realities and discern a faithful response amid complexity by following the persistent example of Christ.

Engaging Lent in a Challenging World

During Lent, we are called not only to self-examination but also to grapple with pressing questions that arise in the intersection of scripture and present-day realities. As we meditate on deliverance, grace, restoration, and promise—anchored in passages such as Exodus 34 and Ezekiel 36—we are challenged to confront the realities of a world shaped by profit-driven systems, including the military and prison industrial complexes, that often marginalize and warehouse individuals based on manipulated and vilified ethnic profiles.

Day 1 (Ash Wednesday)

Drop the Mic

By Dr. Lewis E. Logan, II

Scripture:

> Isaiah 58:1-12, Joel 2:1-2, 12-17 or Psalm 51:1-17;
> 2 Corinthians 5:20b-6:10; Matthew 6:1-6, 16-21

The origin of the expression "drop the mic" is as obscure as the meaning is clear and applicable at the outset of this particularly pivotal 21st-century Lenten Season. The closest reference of note in recent history is former President Barack Obama's final White House Correspondents' Dinner on May 1, 2016, where, after half an hour of political satire, he famously paused, said "Obama out," and dropped the mic.

Of the passages set before us—Joel 2:1-2, 12-17; Psalm 51:1-17; 2 Corinthians 5:20b-6:10; Matthew 6:1-6, 16-21, and Isaiah 58:1-12—I hear the echo of that figurative mic drop in the emphatic voice of the eighth-century prophetic tradition. Their words carry the same weight today: a call to authenticity, to sincerity, and to a deliberate setting aside of the comfort of rote personal agendas for the next forty days towards what we hope will be transformational discipleship.

"We have fasted before you!" they say.
"Why aren't you impressed?
We have been very hard on ourselves,
and you don't even notice it!"

"I will tell you why!" I respond.
"It's because you are fasting to please yourselves.
Even while you fast,
you keep oppressing your workers.

What good is fasting
when you keep on fighting and quarreling?
This kind of fasting
will never get you anywhere with me.

You humble yourselves
by going through the motions of penance,
bowing your heads
like reeds bending in the wind.
You dress in burlap
and cover yourselves with ashes.
Is this what you call fasting?
Do you really think this will please the Lord?

"No, this is the kind of fasting I want:
Free those who are wrongly imprisoned;
lighten the burden of those who work for you.
Let the oppressed go free,
and remove the chains that bind people.

Share your food with the hungry,
and give shelter to the homeless.
Give clothes to those who need them,
and do not hide from relatives who need your help.

"Then your salvation will come like the dawn,
and your wounds will quickly heal.
Your godliness will lead you forward,
and the glory of the Lord will protect you from behind.

Then when you call, the Lord will answer.
"Yes, I am here," he will quickly reply.
"Remove the heavy yoke of oppression.
Stop pointing your finger and spreading vicious rumors!

Feed the hungry,
and help those in trouble.
Then your light will shine out from the darkness,
and the darkness around you
will be as bright as noon."

Isaiah 58:3-10 (NLT)

… Mic drops …

Prayer

At the outset in this new beginning, I want more than the same old religious ritual observance of Lent. This time, Lord, I ask you to help me follow your Holy Spirit to another level of relationship with you. Lord, let the end of this Lenten journey be the harbinger of transformational discipleship in the way that the Apostle Paul describes in Romans 12:1-2 and Philippians 3:10-14.

Amen and *Ase'* (so be it, pronounced ah-SHAY).

Reflection

Watch the YouTube video below and consider the words of Tramaine Hawkins in her 1979 song "Holy One": "I never want to let you down."[1]

---

[1] Tramaine Hawkins, "Holy One," live performance, 1979, YouTube video, 5:32, posted by Vintage Gospel Music, March 12, 2015, https://www.youtube.com/watch?v=QAblVfKrHPg.

Day 2 (Thursday)

Forgiveness

By Bishop Sharma D. Lewis Logan

Scripture:

Psalm 51:1-2 (NKJV)

Have mercy upon me, O God,
According to Your lovingkindness;
According to the multitude of Your tender mercies,
Blot out my transgressions.
Wash me thoroughly from my iniquity,
And cleanse me from my sin.

Psalm 51, a psalm of David, was written after the recorded incident in 2 Samuel 11–12, when the Prophet Nathan confronted David about committing adultery with Bathsheba and murdering Uriah. David writes this psalm confessing his sinful nature and asking God for forgiveness.

According to *Nelson's New Illustrated Bible Dictionary,* "Sin refers to missing the mark," and "forgiveness is the act of excusing or pardoning others despite their shortcoming and errors."[2]

---

[2] Donald F. Youngblood, F. F. Bruce, and R. K. Harrison, *Nelson's New Illustrated Bible Dictionary* (Nashville: Thomas Nelson, 1995), s.v. "Sin," s.v. "Forgiveness."

How many times in our lives do we need to forgive others? Have you ever been so discouraged that you did not want to forgive because there was a violation of trust in the relationship?

As we approach this Lenten Season, the Apostle Paul reminds us in this text that David humbled himself, confessed his sins, and asked God for forgiveness.

According to Professor Kenneth J. Collins, we must understand that "forgiveness may not lead to reconciliation, but it can lead to significant physical, emotional, and spiritual healing for the forgiver as several studies have shown."[3] According to some researchers, forgiveness involves rooting out one's negative thoughts, feelings, and behaviors directed at an offender and developing positive thoughts, feelings, and behaviors towards the offender. United Methodist Pastor Donald Shelby maintains that "forgiveness entails an intentional decision to change how we feel about what happened and what it means to us."

"Forgiveness is also characterized as God's pardon of the sins of human beings."[4] As people of God, we must continue to practice the spirit of forgiveness because we know that forgiveness is directly linked to Jesus Christ.

---

[3] Kenneth J. Collins, *The Theology of John Wesley: Holy Love and the Shape of Grace* (Nashville: Abingdon Press, 2007).

[4] Youngblood, Bruce, and Harrison, *Nelson's New Illustrated Bible Dictionary*, s.v. "Forgiveness."

His sacrificial death on the cross and his resurrection prove this point. God's forgiveness of humanity demands that we forgive others, as grace brings with it responsibility and obligation. As people of God, we are required to forgive those who sin against us.

The Apostle Paul writes in Colossians 3:13 (NKJV): "Bearing with one another and forgiving one another, if anyone has a complaint against another. Even as Christ forgave you, so you also must do." "Bearing with" others involves fully accepting people for who they are, accepting their faults, their flaws, and their shortcomings, and allowing them to be themselves. The problem with us as human beings is that we have a desire to change people to fit our personalities. Why do we think we can hold onto unforgiveness when the Bible clearly states that if we expect to be forgiven by God, then we must walk in the posture of forgiving others? "For if you forgive other people when they sin against you, your heavenly Father will also forgive you. But if you do not forgive others their sins, your Father will not forgive your sins" (Matthew 6:14-15, NIV).

Prayer

Lord, please forgive me, for I have sinned against you.

Amen.

Reflection

Meditate on the forgiveness you have received as a direct link from our Savior dying on the cross.

Day 3 (Friday)

Confessions of a Prophetic Hitman

Dr. Lewis E. Logan, II

Scripture:

Jonah 4:1-11 (NLT)

This change of plans greatly upset Jonah, and he became very angry. So he complained to the Lord about it: "Didn't I say before I left home that you would do this, Lord? That is why I ran away to Tarshish! I knew that you are a merciful and compassionate God, slow to get angry and filled with unfailing love. You are eager to turn back from destroying people. Just kill me now, Lord! I'd rather be dead than alive if what I predicted will not happen."

The Lord replied, "Is it right for you to be angry about this?"

Then Jonah went out to the east side of the city and made a shelter to sit under as he waited to see what would happen to the city. And the Lord God arranged for a leafy plant to grow there, and soon it spread its broad leaves over Jonah's head, shading him from the sun. This eased his discomfort, and Jonah was very grateful for the plant.

But God also arranged for a worm! The next morning at dawn the worm ate through the stem of the plant so that it withered away. 8 And as the sun grew hot, God arranged for a scorching east wind to blow on Jonah. The sun beat down on his head until he grew faint and wished to die. "Death is certainly better than living like this!" he exclaimed.

Then God said to Jonah, "Is it right for you to be angry because the plant died?"

"Yes," Jonah retorted, "even angry enough to die!"

Then the Lord said, "You feel sorry about the plant, though you did nothing to put it there. It came quickly and died quickly. But Nineveh has more than 120,000 people living in spiritual darkness,[a] not to mention all the animals. Shouldn't I feel sorry for such a great city?"

Confessions of a Prophetic Hitman

Sharing the following confessions of a prophetic hitman brings a measure of relief, and therapeutic honesty. There is within me a profound resentment of governments, individuals in power, organized military operations, and commercial industries that profit from endless wars. I seethe with deep antipathy when I see or hear of genocide, famine, sexual violence as a weapon of war, insensate environmental decimation, and deliberate inhumane deprivation. Their actions, which tear at the fabric of human potential and generate inhumane levels of scarcity, persistent poverty, environmental toxification, food insecurity, and ruthless corruption, prompt me to the struggle and solace of self-disclosure, and even my own complicity.

Complicity and Corporate Influence

The scale of this complicity is staggering, particularly the connection between the military-industrial complex, global capital, and corporate-controlled media. These profit-driven forces spread propaganda and orchestrate manipulative narratives that mislead the public and pacify stockholders. Corporations and nations alike deploy their resources to battlefields, treating them as marketplaces for the latest technologies of mass destruction and distraction.

These tools, showcased to the highest bidders, introduce new levels of precision and devastation. This relentless cycle drains resources that could foster human development and wellbeing, replacing them with chaos and confusion.

Our demand for apparel, cars, jewelry, food, luxury excursions, and our tech gadgets, games, cellphones, and computers – all spoils of global capital – makes us a part of a comprehensive cloud of unabashed complicity. Notice the *our?* Can you hear me now?

Listen to: Jonathan McReynolds...pay particular attention to the final verse "forgive when I'm one of those people...deliver me."[5]

Reflections on Peace and Mercy

The longing for divine judgment and peace persists within me, echoing the biblical prophetic hitman Jonah, a figure defined by contradiction. Jonah's name, which means "dove," stands for peace, yet he was consumed by disdain for Assyrian imperial power, circumnavigating his divine calling while craving retribution.

---

[5] https://youtu.be/6_8d-W_lorY?si=MqD_AId2ohd1Pu78.

Like Jonah, I am all too aware of the terrors of imperial aggression. I share Jonah's anger at God's mercy toward the merciless and see myself reflected in his inner turmoil. I, too, am a prophetic hitman. Yet, the divine question still lingers: Shouldn't there be compassion, even for those living in darkness (Jonah 4:11)?

Judgment, Mercy, and the Challenge of Forgiveness

Imagining forgiveness for war criminals, heads of state, imperialists, and weapons manufacturers—those enriched by endless wars—feels unthinkable. The notion that God could love such individuals unsettles me. Yet, like Jonah, I am forced to face the truth that the same Jesus who died for me also died for them, embracing even those I find hardest to forgive.

The Depths of Mercy

Perhaps in contemplating the true depth of divine mercy, I am struck and transformed by the Prince of Peace, who gave his life for all, inclusive of the perpetrators of violence and those like me. Who am I to judge when such boundless mercy exists? These are honest confessions of someone wrestling with anger, disdain, astonishment, and the limitless reach of sacrifice and forgiveness. Like Jonah's minor musings, these are the confessions of a prophetic hitman.

Prayer

"Through us, and the church, infinite wrong was done. We accuse ourselves for not standing by our beliefs more courageously, for not praying more faithfully, for not believing more joyously, and for not loving more completely."[6]

Amen and Ase'.

Reflection

Silence is violence, especially to our own hypocrisy. Lord, have mercy on us—have mercy on me.

---

[6] *Bonhoeffer: Pastor. Spy. Assassin.* Directed by Todd Komarnicki (Provo, UT: Angel Studios, 2024).

Day 4 (Saturday)

The Childlike Faith

By Bishop Sharma D. Lewis Logan

Scripture:

Matthew 18:1-7 (CEB)

At that time the disciples came to Jesus and asked, "Who is the greatest in the kingdom of heaven?"

Then he called a little child over to sit among the disciples, and said, "I assure you that if you don't turn your lives around and become like this little child, you will definitely not enter the kingdom of heaven. Those who humble themselves like this little child will be the greatest in the kingdom of heaven. Whoever welcomes one such child in my name welcomes me.

"As for whoever causes these little ones who believe in me to trip and fall into sin, it would be better for them to have a huge stone hung around their necks and be drowned in the bottom of the lake. How terrible it is for the world because of the things that cause people to trip and fall into sin! Such things have to happen, but how terrible it is for the person who causes those things to happen!

When I was growing up in Statesboro, Georgia, my mother would often say, "Sharma, you have an old soul and a childlike faith." It wasn't until I was older that I understood these statements. I attributed my learning to the disciplines of memorizing Bible verses, reading God's

Word, and praying, which I learned from my parents, Aunt Essie C. Simmons (who happens to be a United Methodist pastor), and Mrs. Amanda Smith.

As a child, I had an interesting connection with older people, particularly those in my church. I enjoyed my friendship with Mrs. Smith. I could listen to her talk for hours about her upbringing, teaching school, and her love for our church, Brannen Chapel United Methodist Church. I believe my old soul was attributed to my relationship with Mrs. Smith.

My parents, my Aunt Essie, and Mrs. Smith helped to mold my childlike faith. It was normal for me to walk from my parents' business on Saturdays and assist Mrs. Smith in preparing for our Sunday school lesson. When I visited her on Saturdays, she would normally have teacakes, in the oven that I couldn't wait to eat with milk. Our Saturday ritual consisted of me telling her about my week, learning a new Bible verse, and listening to her many stories. On Sunday mornings, I always enjoyed being in her class.

Mrs. Smith had a unique way of teaching us the Bible stories. And if we participated and behaved, she would always reward us with peppermint sticks and candy corns wrapped in tissue that was always stuck together in her purse.

In today's text, to enter the Kingdom of God, we must have a childlike spirit. Jesus begins with a question from his disciples: Who is the greatest in the kingdom? Calling over a child to stand among them, Jesus declares that if his followers do not change and become like that child, they will not enter the kingdom. To change means to repent. The biblical definition of "repentance" means to change one's mind and heart about sin.

Interestingly, children were not highly valued in antiquity, but Jesus makes the point that his followers must have a humble spirit like that of a child. In the Bible, "humility" is defined as a virtue characterized by a modest view of oneself and a recognition of one's dependence on God. There are several examples of humility expressed in the Bible: Jesus washing the disciples' feet, Mary washing Jesus' feet with her hair, and Job, despite his suffering, maintaining his trust in God when his wife and friends turned their backs on him.

As a child, I learned that I could trust only God and my parents. At a young age, I was taught to be open to the presence and move of God. I attributed this teaching to my Apostolic and Pentecostal aunts, who reminded me often that when we approached the altar, we were to "tarry" until the Holy Spirit fell upon us. I respected what they said, and as a result of "tarrying," I witnessed at an early age people speaking in tongues, being slayed in the Spirit, and holy dancing.

I challenge you during this Lenten season to approach God with a childlike faith—believing, trusting, and obeying God's Word. It was English author Samuel Butler who once said, "You can do very little with faith, but can do nothing without it."[7]

Prayer

O Lord, help me to possess a childlike faith to enter the Kingdom of Heaven.

Amen.

Reflection

How do we teach our children to respond to the move of God?

_____

_____

_____

_____

_____

---

[7] Samuel Butler, *The Notebooks of Samuel Butler, Part XXI*, "Success," (1912), quoted in Goodreads (accessed August 25, 2025), https://www.goodreads.com/quotes/260055-you-can-do-very-little-with-faith-but-you-can.

Day 5 (Monday)

He is Like Us

By Dr. Lewis E. Logan, II

Scripture:

Hebrews 2:14-18 (NLT)

Because God's children are human beings—made of flesh and blood—the Son also became flesh and blood. For only as a human being could he die, and only by dying could he break the power of the devil, who had[a] the power of death. Only in this way could he set free all who have lived their lives as slaves to the fear of dying.

We also know that the Son did not come to help angels; he came to help the descendants of Abraham. Therefore, it was necessary for him to be made in every respect like us, his brothers and sisters, so that he could be our merciful and faithful High Priest before God. Then he could offer a sacrifice that would take away the sins of the people. Since he himself has gone through suffering and testing, he is able to help us when we are being tested.

Christ's Humanity and Sacrifice

Hebrews 2:14-18 reveals that because God's children are made of flesh and blood, the Son also became fully human. Only by becoming human could Jesus experience death and thereby break the power of the devil, who once held the power of death. This act set free all who had lived their lives enslaved by the fear of dying.

Christ did not come to help angels but to help the descendants of Abraham. He needed to be made like us in every way, so he could become a merciful and faithful High Priest before God, offering a sacrifice to take away the sins of the people. Because Jesus himself suffered and was tested, he is able to help us in our times of testing.

Comparison to Greek Gods

For years, I have listened to Dr. Bill Creasy's commentary on the Pauline Epistles. He often draws a profound contrast between the Greek gods and the God of Jehovah. In his view, the gods of Greek mythology never sacrificed their divinity to experience the fullness of the human condition like Jehovah God did through Jesus.

While gods like Zeus, Aries, and Apollo are depicted in art and legend, they do not become like us—they do not bleed, suffer, or die as we do. Dr. Creasy emphasizes that this is not only because the Greek gods are fictional but also because the true God, through Jesus, entered fully into our experience. God in Jesus "thought it not robbery" to lay aside divinity and take on humanity (Philippians 2:5-11). The Greek gods do not die as we do, but Jesus did.

Jesus' Solidarity with Humanity

The author of Hebrews, addressing a community under siege, highlights this distinct difference: Jesus is like us. His suffering for our sake forms an internal and eternal bond—we suffer with Jesus, and he suffers with us. The refrain from Kendrick Lamar's 2024 song "They're Not Like Us" echoes this truth: the gods of legend are not like us, but Jesus is. Because Jesus experienced weakness and testing, he is able to help us when we, too, are being tested. His grace, forgiveness, empathy, and mercy are available to all of us who seek deliverance from and fellowship in our suffering.

Prayer

I get that you get me, Lord, and that gives me hope. I see that you see me, Jesus, and that sources my self-esteem. The fact that you're feeling me is a sunshine smile to my soul. And this joy I have, the world can't give it, and the world can't take it away!

Amen and Ase.'

Reflection

Here's mystery and destiny: God became like us to show us how to become more like God.

Day 6 (Tuesday)

Forgiveness

By Bishop Sharma D. Lewis Logan

Scripture:

Psalm 32 (NIV)

*Blessed is the one whose transgressions are forgiven,
 whose sins are covered.
Blessed is the one whose sin the Lord does not count
against them and in whose spirit is no deceit.*

*When I kept silent, my bones wasted away through my
groaning all day long.
For day and night your hand was heavy on me;
my strength was sapped as in the heat of summer.*

*Then I acknowledged my sin to you and did not cover up
my iniquity.
I said, "I will confess my transgressions to the Lord."
And you forgave the guilt of my sin.*

*Therefore let all the faithful pray to you while you may
be found; surely the rising of the mighty waters will not
reach them.*

*You are my hiding place; you will protect me from trouble
and surround me with songs of deliverance.*

*I will instruct you and teach you in the way you should go;
I will counsel you with my loving eye on you.
Do not be like the horse or the mule, which have no
understanding
but must be controlled by bit and bridle or they will not
come to you.*

Many are the woes of the wicked, but the Lord's unfailing love surrounds the one who trusts in him.

Rejoice in the Lord and be glad, you righteous; sing, all you who are upright in heart!

Psalm 32 is known as a Penitential Psalm, highlighting the theme of forgiveness and repentance. There are two main themes in Psalm 32: the blessing that comes from confessing sin and the joy of receiving God's forgiveness.

According to *Nelson's Bible Dictionary*, "Forgiveness is characterized as God's pardon of the sins of human beings."[8] As believers, we must continue to practice forgiveness because we know that forgiveness is deeply rooted in the teachings of Jesus Christ. His life, his sacrificial death on the cross, and his resurrection prove this point. William Blake reminds us that "the glory of Christianity is to conquer by forgiveness."[9]

God forgives sinners because forgiveness has always been a part of God's loving character. As believers, we are to model forgiveness for those who sin against us. Archbishop Desmond Tutu stated, "Forgiving is not forgetting; it's actually remembering—remembering and not using your right to hit back."[10]

---

[8] *Nelson's New Illustrated Bible Dictionary*, s.v. "Forgiveness."

[9] William Blake, *The Complete Poetry and Prose of William Blake*, ed. David V. Erdman, rev. ed. (Berkeley: University of California Press, 1982), 665.

[10] Desmond Tutu, *No Future Without Forgiveness* (New York: Doubleday, 1999), 219.

Jesus' illustration is prompted by Peter, who asks how many times we should forgive. Peter believes that seven times is enough. However, Jesus answers by saying, "Seventy-seven times" (Matthew 18:22, NIV), revealing to us that true forgiveness has no boundaries or limits.

As we examine the text, David declares in Psalm 32:1-5 the need to confess our sins. Scripture encourages us in 1 John 1:9 (NIV), "If we confess our sins, he is faithful and just and will forgive us our sins and purify us from all unrighteousness."

David speaks in Psalm 32:6-7 that unconfessed sin harms our spiritual souls. Finally, in verses 8-11, the reader acknowledges that trusting God's wisdom and being obedient to God's instructions restores our relationship with God as we seek forgiveness.

Prayer

O Lord, give me the strength to confess my faults before you.

Amen.

Reflection

What happens to our spiritual souls when we have unconfessed sin?

Day 7 (Wednesday)

From Refusal to Release

By Dr. Lewis E. Logan, II

Scripture:

Psalm 32:3-5 (NLT)

When I refused to confess my sin,
  my body wasted away,
  and I groaned all day long.
Day and night your hand of discipline was heavy on me.
  My strength evaporated like water in the summer heat.
Finally, I confessed all my sins to you
  and stopped trying to hide my guilt.
I said to myself, "I will confess my rebellion to the Lord."
  And you forgave me! All my guilt is gone.

The Discipline of Spiritual Release

There exists a spiritual discipline within discipleship that is often overlooked or underdeveloped. We may never fully master it—indeed, spiritual growth is a lifelong process—but recognizing its importance remains crucial. Dr. David A. Seamands, in his book "Healing for Damaged Emotions," emphasizes the value of being fully known,[11] a lesson echoed in King David's words in Psalm 51.

This discipline involves confession and the intentional release of our inner burdens, much like the lesson learned at the pivotal moment described in 2 Samuel 11. Because God already knows our every thought, whether noble or flawed, choosing to release these thoughts prevents the internal pressure that comes from hiding or refusing to acknowledge them.

We invite deeper intimacy with God by not "wearing the mask" as poet Paul Laurence Dunbar described in his 1865 cryptic musing. Practicing continual release, knowing that we are already known, brings a peace reminiscent of Paul's admonition in Philippians 4:6-7 "Don't worry about anything…" (NLT)

Don't worry about anything; instead, pray about everything. Tell God what you need, and thank him for all he has done. Then you will experience God's peace, which exceeds anything we can understand. His peace will guard your hearts and minds as you live in Christ Jesus.

Prayer

Thank you, Lord, for allowing me to learn that anxious feelings are your open invitations to immediately and constantly tell you everything I'm facing, feeling, or even

---

[11] David A. Seamands, *Healing for Damaged Emotions* (Wheaton, IL: Victor Books, 1981).

fearing. I so appreciate the peace you give me when I come just as I am, no matter what I've done or am going through. The peace and power I experience never cease to blow my mind. I'm grateful that through all of this, I'm learning to love, trust, follow, and serve you!

Amen and Ase'.

Reflection

Augustine the African Bishop of Antiquity, wrote:

"You have made us for yourself, Lord, and our hearts are restless until they rest in you."[12]

From *The Mask,*[13] by Paul Laurence Dunbar:

> *We smile, but, O great Christ, our cries,*
> *To thee from tortured souls arise.*
> *We sing, but oh the clay is vile*
> *Beneath our feet, and long the mile.*
> *But let the world dream otherwise,*
> *We wear the mask!*

---

[12] Augustine of Hippo, *Confessions*, trans. Henry Chadwick (Oxford: Oxford University Press, 1991), 3.

[13] Paul Laurence Dunbar, *We Wear the Mask.*

Day 8 (Thursday)

My Help

By Bishop Sharma D. Lewis Logan

Scripture:

Psalm 121 (NIV)

*I lift up my eyes to the mountains—
where does my help come from?*

*My help comes from the Lord,
the Maker of heaven and earth.*

*He will not let your foot slip—
he who watches over you will not slumber;*

*indeed, he who watches over Israel
will neither slumber nor sleep.*

*The Lord watches over you—
the Lord is your shade at your right hand;*

*the sun will not harm you by day,
nor the moon by night.*

*The Lord will keep you from all harm—
he will watch over your life;*

*the Lord will watch over your coming and going
both now and forevermore.*

As long as I can remember, "my help" has always come from my Lord and Savior. My parents raised us to help our family, help people who are less fortunate than us, and know assuredly that we could always count on God. My parents grounded our upbringing on reading God's Word, attending church every Sunday, and establishing a strong prayer life. I knew without a shadow of doubt that if my parents couldn't help me, God would always be there to help. Hebrews 13:5 (NIV) shares a powerful promise: "God will never leave you nor forsake you."

Psalm 121 is a song for pilgrims ascending to Jerusalem. Some scholars believe that Hebrew pilgrims may have sung songs of ascents found in Psalms 120–134 as they traveled to Jerusalem to celebrate one of the Old Testament's annual worship festivals.

The text for this morning raises the crucial question, "Where does my help come from?" With a reply, "My help comes from the Lord, who made heaven and earth!"

As children, my siblings and I were raised to totally depend on and trust in God. My parents—as they worked, sacrificed, and saved for all six of us to graduate from college—instilled in us the belief that God would always take care of us. My dad strongly believed that God's presence and faithfulness would always be with us, even in difficult times.

In 1955, my parents started their first business, Lewis Van Lines. They then opened Lewis Mart & Carousel Drive-In in 1967 in Statesboro, Georgia. Can you imagine an African American man with a high school certificate who had the courage and fortitude to start his own business with my mother as his partner and bookkeeper?

My father, once a bartender at the Statesboro Country Club, embodied the belief in this text that his Lord and Savior was his present help. I remember my parents combining their money, dreaming out loud, and believing that one day they would have their own businesses that would leave a legacy for our family.

Ever since I was blessed to be elected as a bishop in The United Methodist Church, I have relied on this text during challenging times and when making difficult decisions that were not always welcomed in the conference or the Church.

As a believer, I've found assurance in Psalm 121:8 (NIV), "The Lord will watch over your coming and going both now and forevermore."

I've come to recognize from this text that my Lord and Savior is my helper, guardian, protector, and shepherd who never sleeps or slumbers. Psalm 46:1 (NIV) reminds us, "God is our refuge and strength, an ever-present help in times of trouble."

Prayer

O Lord, I have come to know you as my ever-present helper!

Amen.

Reflection

How has the Lord been a helper, guardian, protector, and shepherd who never sleeps or slumbers?

Day 9 (Friday)

Awesome!

By Dr. Lewis E. Logan, II

Scripture:

Micah 7 (NLT)

How miserable I am!
I feel like the fruit picker after the harvest
   who can find nothing to eat.
Not a cluster of grapes or a single early fig
   can be found to satisfy my hunger.
The godly people have all disappeared;
   not one honest person is left on the earth.
They are all murderers,
   setting traps even for their own brothers.
Both their hands are equally skilled at doing evil!
   Officials and judges alike demand bribes.
The people with influence get what they want,
   and together they scheme to twist justice.
Even the best of them is like a brier;
   the most honest is as dangerous as a hedge of thorns.
But your judgment day is coming swiftly now.
   Your time of punishment is here, a time of confusion.
Don't trust anyone—
   not your best friend or even your wife!
For the son despises his father.
   The daughter defies her mother.
The daughter-in-law defies her mother-in-law.
   Your enemies are right in your own household!

As for me, I look to the Lord for help.
   I wait confidently for God to save me,
   and my God will certainly hear me.

Do not gloat over me, my enemies!
  For though I fall, I will rise again.
Though I sit in darkness,
  the Lord will be my light.
I will be patient as the Lord punishes me,
  for I have sinned against him.
But after that, he will take up my case
  and give me justice for all I have suffered from my enemies.
The Lord will bring me into the light,
  and I will see his righteousness.
Then my enemies will see that the Lord is on my side.
  They will be ashamed that they taunted me, saying,
"So where is the Lord—
  that God of yours?"
With my own eyes I will see their downfall;
  they will be trampled like mud in the streets.
In that day, Israel, your cities will be rebuilt,
  and your borders will be extended.
People from many lands will come and honor you—
  from Assyria all the way to the towns of Egypt,
from Egypt all the way to the Euphrates River,[a]
  and from distant seas and mountains.
But the land will become empty and desolate
  because of the wickedness of those who live there.
O Lord, protect your people with your shepherd's staff;
  lead your flock, your special possession.
Though they live alone in a thicket
  on the heights of Mount Carmel,[c]
let them graze in the fertile pastures of Bashan and Gilead
  as they did long ago.
"Yes," says the Lord,
  "I will do mighty miracles for you,
like those I did when I rescued you
  from slavery in Egypt."
All the nations of the world will stand amazed
  at what the Lord will do for you.
They will be embarrassed
  at their feeble power.
They will cover their mouths in silent awe,
  deaf to everything around them.

> *Like snakes crawling from their holes,*
> > *they will come out to meet the Lord our God.*
> *They will fear him greatly,*
> > *trembling in terror at his presence.*
> *Where is another God like you,*
> > *who pardons the guilt of the remnant,*
> > *overlooking the sins of his special people?*
> *You will not stay angry with your people forever,*
> > *because you delight in showing unfailing love.*
> *Once again you will have compassion on us.*
> > *You will trample our sins under your feet*
> > *and throw them into the depths of the ocean!*
> *You will show us your faithfulness and unfailing love*
> > *as you promised to our ancestors Abraham and Jacob*
> > *long ago.*

The eighth-century prophet Micah, who may have been a contemporary of Isaiah, engages with the rhetorical implications of his name, which means "Who is like God?" as referenced in verse 18. When he considers the countless admonitions and aspirations God sent him to pronounce in Chapters 1–6, Micah had to admit by Chapter 7 that a God who would put up with such corrupt, rebellious, wicked, idolatrous, and unfaithful people by insisting on keeping the promised Abrahamic Covenant is absolutely awesome.

Like Micah, we witness such stark parallels and paradoxes from various media. Depending upon your perspective, you may even experience similar discomfort (verses 1, 8). Yet, we are offered the opportunity Micah embraced. Verse 7 suggests an homage to the venerated 20th-century theologian Karl Barth: "Take your Bible and take your newspaper, and read both. But interpret newspapers from your Bible."[14] Ultimately, our hope is in our Awesome God, whom we trust in prayerful anticipation, prophetic pronouncement, and persistent praxis.

Prayer

"O LORD, protect your people with your shepherd's staff; lead your flock, your special possession. Though they live alone in a thicket on the heights of Mount Carmel, let them graze in the fertile pastures of Bashan and Gilead as they did long ago" (Micah 7:14, NLT).

Amen and Ase'.

Reflection

Love so amazing, so divine,
Demands my soul, my life, my all.[15]

---

[14] Karl Barth, "Barth in Retirement," *Time*, May 31, 1963, 70.

[15] Isaac Watts, "When I Survey the Wondrous Cross," 1707; *The African Methodist Episcopal Hymnal* (Nashville: African Methodist Episcopal Church, 2011), no. 147; and *The United Methodist Hymnal* (Nashville: United Methodist Publishing House, 1989), nos. 298–99.

Day 10 (Saturday)

The Gentiles' Faith

By Bishop Sharma D. Lewis Logan

Scripture:

Luke 7:1-10 (NIV)

When Jesus had finished saying all this to the people who were listening, he entered Capernaum. There a centurion's servant, whom his master valued highly, was sick and about to die. The centurion heard of Jesus and sent some elders of the Jews to him, asking him to come and heal his servant. When they came to Jesus, they pleaded earnestly with him, "This man deserves to have you do this, because he loves our nation and has built our synagogue." So Jesus went with them.

He was not far from the house when the centurion sent friends to say to him: "Lord, don't trouble yourself, for I do not deserve to have you come under my roof. That is why I did not even consider myself worthy to come to you. But say the word, and my servant will be healed. For I myself am a man under authority, with soldiers under me. I tell this one, 'Go,' and he goes; and that one, 'Come,' and he comes. I say to my servant, 'Do this,' and he does it."

When Jesus heard this, he was amazed at him, and turning to the crowd following him, he said, "I tell you, I have not found such great faith even in Israel." Then the men who had been sent returned to the house and found the servant well.

Hebrews 11:1 (NKJV) states, "Now faith is the substance of things hoped for, the evidence of things not seen." Throughout Luke's Gospel and the Book of Acts, we witness the common thread of "faith." As believers, our faith is tried and tested every day. The Epistle of James 1:2-3 (NIV) reiterates, "Consider it pure joy, my brothers and sisters, whenever you face trials of many kinds, because you know that the testing of your faith produces perseverance."

As we read the Bible, we encounter numerous references on the topic of faith. By faith, Abraham obeyed and left his country; by faith, the woman who had suffered with bleeding was healed by a simple touch, and by faith, the centurion asked Jesus to heal his servant—by speaking from afar. It is known in Luke's writings that the believing centurions represented all Gentiles who became God-fearers.

Faith is vital to all aspects of the believer's life. As Mother Teresa once said, "Be faithful in small things because it is in them that your strength lies." Gospel singer Mahalia Jackson stated that "faith and prayer are the vitamins of the soul; man cannot live in health without them."[16] The hymn "We've Come This Far by Faith," written by Albert A. Goodson, has long brought comfort to my soul, reminding me to lean on the Lord and trust his unfailing Word.[17]

There are three lessons we can learn from today's

---

[16] Mahalia Jackson, Mahalia Jackson: *The Power and the Glory*, ed. Jesse Jackson (New York: Ballantine Books, 1993), 114.

[17] Albert A. Goodson, *We've Come This Far by Faith* (Los Angeles: Manna Music, 1965).

text. First, in Luke 7:1-5, the centurion officer made a bold request that Jesus come and heal his servant. The centurion officer knew he was unworthy for Jesus to come to the home of a Gentile. However, he stood on his faith that Jesus could heal his servant. Secondly, the centurion reveals in verses 6-9 that he believed Jesus could speak the healing from afar. Finally, the centurion's faith was rewarded with an immediate healing in verse 10. The Savior's physical presence was not required. Jesus' word was enough. When we face problems, is God's Word enough to get us through our situation?

Prayer

O Lord, your Word is more than enough.

Amen.

Reflection

Meditate on several healing stories in the Bible. Do you recognize the common thread of faith in each story?

Day 11 (Monday)

"SMH" (Shaking My Head)

By Dr. Lewis E. Logan, II

Scripture:

Numbers 21:4-9 (NLT)

> *They traveled from Mount Hor along the route to the Red Sea, to go around Edom. But the people grew impatient on the way; they spoke against God and against Moses, and said, "Why have you brought us up out of Egypt to die in the wilderness? There is no bread! There is no water! And we detest this miserable food!"*
>
> *Then the Lord sent venomous snakes among them; they bit the people and many Israelites died. The people came to Moses and said, "We sinned when we spoke against the Lord and against you. Pray that the Lord will take the snakes away from us." So Moses prayed for the people.*
>
> *The Lord said to Moses, "Make a snake and put it up on a pole; anyone who is bitten can look at it and live." So Moses made a bronze snake and put it up on a pole. Then when anyone was bitten by a snake and looked at the bronze snake, they lived.*

All I could do was shake my head after reading this passage, remarking, "How ironic is this?" Since I was a teenager, I have read scripture daily, but never until this opportunity to share this reflection with you in excellence have I experienced a different kind of "PTSD," "People

Traumatic Scripture Dilemma" moment. If you're a servant leader in people-oriented organizations, you may need to talk with your therapist as I do when those you lead turn against you, on the one hand, and then turn back to you, on the other.

It is far too common for individuals to praise leaders when all is well but to scold, condemn, and vilify them during difficulties. Jepthah, the ninth judge of Israel, must have shaken his head as he listened in disbelief to the same voices who ostracized him for being the product of his father's indiscretion with a harlot, on one hand, now asking for his protection against the Ammonites.

Seeking God's guidance on how to provide servant leadership when unpopular at best and under attack at worst is imperative. Further, how do leaders serve those whose desperate appeals for help are as impassioned as their preceding vitriol? Listening attentively to and maintaining a sense of connection to one's guiding principles are essential skills. Forgiving offensive comments and behavior is a difficult yet necessary discipline that builds fortitude, character, and resolve.

According to Matthew 5:11-12 (NLT), Jesus, the ultimate Moses, admonishes us to respond to adversity with patience and prayer, drawing inspiration from our prophetic predecessors: "God blesses you when people mock you and persecute you and lie about you and say all sorts of evil things against you because you are my followers. Be happy about it! Be very glad! For a great reward awaits you in heaven. And remember, the ancient prophets were persecuted in the same way".

Perhaps we may be inspired and encouraged to redefine the acronym "SMH," meaning "Shaking My Head," to "Secure My Hope" or "Secure My Help."

Prayer

Lord, I lift up to you my anger and frustration of serving recalcitrant, negative, and downright disrespectful people as an evening offering (Psalm 141:2) of gratitude and trust. I give the situation and the individuals to you one by one, name by name. Thank you, Lord, for challenging personalities and circumstances that encourage my prayer life. Please forgive me, Lord, especially when I'm one of those people.

Amen and Ase'.

Reflection

Difficulties are drivers of diligence, determination, and disclosure.

But in that coming day no weapon turned against you will succeed. You will silence every voice raised up to accuse you. These benefits are enjoyed by the servants of the Lord; their vindication will come from me. I, the Lord, have spoken!

Isaiah 54:17 (NLT)

Day 12 (Tuesday)

Facing Death

By Bishop Sharma D. Lewis Logan

Scripture:

Isaiah 65:17-25 (NIV)

"See, I will create new heavens and a new earth.
The former things will not be remembered, nor will they come to mind.
But be glad and rejoice forever in what I will create,
for I will create Jerusalem to be a delight and its people a joy.
I will rejoice over Jerusalem and take delight in my people;
the sound of weeping and of crying will be heard in it no more.
"Never again will there be in it an infant who lives but a few days, or an old man who does not live out his years;
the one who dies at a hundred will be thought a mere child;
the one who fails to reach a hundred will be considered accursed.
They will build houses and dwell in them; they will plant vineyards and eat their fruit.
No longer will they build houses and others live in them, or plant and others eat.
For as the days of a tree, so will be the days of my people;
my chosen ones will long enjoy the work of their hands.
They will not labor in vain, nor will they bear children doomed to misfortune;

for they will be a people blessed by the Lord, they and their descendants with them.
Before they call I will answer; while they are still speaking I will hear.
The wolf and the lamb will feed together, and the lion will eat straw like the ox, and dust will be the serpent's food. They will neither harm nor destroy on all my holy mountain," says the Lord.

The text for today, Isaiah 65:17-25, parallels Revelation 21:5 (NIV): "Then I saw 'a new heaven and a new earth,' for the first heaven and the first earth had passed away, and there was no longer any sea. I saw the Holy City, the new Jerusalem coming down out of heaven from God."

In the new heaven and earth, God will remove all suffering revealed in Revelation 7:16 (NIV), "Never again will they hunger, never again will they thirst. The sun will not beat down on them, nor any scorching heat."

Both scriptures in Isaiah and Revelation bring comfort, because out of the new heaven comes a new city, the eternal rest of the redeemed, where God lives with God's saints. According to scholars, heaven will wipe away five aspects of the human experience: death, mourning, tears, crying, and pain.

I have always found death and dying intriguing, as I've lost several loved ones to tragic car accidents, cancer, complications from surgery, and simply old age. The most profound experience in losing loved ones was when my Aunt Essie, my great-uncle BJ, my sister Wanda, and my father all passed in a span of sixteen months. Life didn't seem fair, but the eternal reward was waiting for each of them. They all lived fulfilled and courageous lives and had a personal relationship with Jesus Christ. As we mourn, we come to recognize as believers that this life is temporary and transitional.

I have found that the passage of scripture for today's meditation brings great strength and comfort to families during this difficult time, because in heaven, there will be no more hardship or sorrow. Isaiah 65:17-18 (NIV) reads:

> *See, I will create new heavens and a new earth. The former things will not be remembered, nor will they come to mind. But be glad and rejoice forever in what I will create, for I will create Jerusalem to be a delight and its people a joy.*

HarperCollins Bible Commentary states, "The prophet Isaiah has described the pictorial image of the new heavens and the new earth. The creation of a new heaven and earth refers to God as the one who 'creates' new things past and present."[18] Today's text emphasizes a future of peace and the absence of grief where God's people will participate in the rejoicing.

Prayer

O Lord, you alone decide life and death. Be gracious to your servants who believe in you.

Amen.

---

[18] *The HarperCollins Bible Commentary,* James L. Mays., Rev. ed. (San Francisco: HarperSanFrancisco, 2000).

Reflection

What scriptures bring you comfort in the times of death and dying?

Day 13 (Wednesday)

The Ultimate Finisher

By Dr. Lewis E. Logan, II

Scripture:

Ezekiel 36:22-32 (NLT)

Therefore, give the people of Israel this message from the Sovereign Lord: I am bringing you back, but not because you deserve it. I am doing it to protect my holy name, on which you brought shame while you were scattered among the nations. I will show how holy my great name is—the name on which you brought shame among the nations. And when I reveal my holiness through you before their very eyes, says the Sovereign Lord, then the nations will know that I am the Lord. For I will gather you up from all the nations and bring you home again to your land.

"Then I will sprinkle clean water on you, and you will be clean. Your filth will be washed away, and you will no longer worship idols. And I will give you a new heart, and I will put a new spirit in you. I will take out your stony, stubborn heart and give you a tender, responsive heart. And I will put my Spirit in you so that you will follow my decrees and be careful to obey my regulations.

"And you will live in Israel, the land I gave your ancestors long ago. You will be my people, and I will be your God. I will cleanse you of your filthy behavior. I will give you good crops of grain, and I will send no more famines on the land. I will give you great harvests from your fruit trees and fields, and never again will the surrounding nations be able to scoff at your land for its famines. Then you will

remember your past sins and despise yourselves for all the detestable things you did. But remember, says the Sovereign Lord, I am not doing this because you deserve it. O my people of Israel, you should be utterly ashamed of all you have done!

A Lesson from Baseball

In another season of life, I played baseball. I was decent—nothing spectacular, but I had pretty good speed and could hold my own at the plate. My greater strength, though, was in defense. I played third base, first base, left field, and occasionally shortstop. My height and long legs gave me an advantage, allowing me to stretch for throws to first base that might otherwise have gone astray.

Sometimes, as the innings wore on, our coach would switch out the pitcher for the final stretch. He always called this new pitcher "the finisher." I remember one "finisher" who threw so hard that every pitch produced a dirt cloud from the catcher's glove. We called him "Smokey" because he threw "smoke." This pitcher was especially trained and prepared to bring fresh energy to close the game. I'm not sure where that player is today or if he ever made it to the big leagues, but on our team, he brought the smoke. He was the finisher.

Whenever I watch baseball now, I find myself looking out for who will step up as the finisher. Yet, as much as I admire these athletes, their skills are dwarfed by what God does.

Ezekiel's Vision: God as the Ultimate Finisher

Ezekiel, both priest and prophet, was deported from his homeland by an imperial power—a king, a dictator—in 596 BCE. He was among the first to be deported, held hostage, and detained. Yet, despite these circumstances, Ezekiel dared to hope. He experienced the presence of God even when he was far from the place God had established, the very place where God had instructed the building of the Ark and the Temple.

Ezekiel's story shows that, beyond exile and historical dislocation, God is not confined to a historic motif, pastime, position, or place. Ezekiel, as both priest and prophet, serves as a minister to God, offering himself as a conduit through whom God can speak. Simultaneously, he spoke to people who needed to hear and be strengthened by the words of the Lord—people who needed to be reminded that even in the presence of brutal occupying forces, God is still present.

God's Glory and Purpose

God gave Ezekiel visions of God's own *kavod*—God's glory/smoke, a weightiness and heaviness that yields discernible presence even in exile. God acts not just out of love for us or because we deserve it but for the sake of God's own name. God is determined, no matter the circumstances, to "bring the smoke"—to finish what was started.

As we continue this Lenten walk—a journey of restoration, renewal, repentance, and re-centering—let us remember the words from Paul in Philippians 1:6 (NLT): "And I am certain that God, who began the good work within you, will continue his work until it is finally finished on the day when Christ Jesus returns." Truly, God is the ultimate finisher.

Prayer

Your ways are higher than my ways (Isaiah 55:8). Lord, please help me get out of my own way as you have your way. As soon as I think I've seen everything, you work out something I never would have imagined.

Amen and Ase'.

Reflection

And I am certain that God, who began the good work within you, will continue his work until it is finally finished on the day when Christ Jesus returns.

Philippians 1:6, NLT

Where there's divine smoke, there's hope.

Day 14 (Thursday)

Worship

By Bishop Sharma D. Lewis Logan

Scripture:

Psalm 95 (CEB)

Come, let us sing to the Lord! Let us shout joyfully to the Rock of our salvation.

Let us come to him with thanksgiving. Let us sing psalms of praise to him.

For the Lord is a great God, a great King above all gods.

He holds in his hands the depths of the earth and the mightiest mountains.

The sea belongs to him, for he made it. His hands formed the dry land, too.

Come, let us worship and bow down. Let us kneel before the Lord our maker, for he is our God.

We are the people he watches over, the flock under his care.

If only you would listen to his voice today!

The Lord says, "Don't harden your hearts as Israel did at Meribah, as they did at Massah in the wilderness.

For there your ancestors tested and tried my patience, even though they saw everything I did.

For forty years I was angry with them, and I said, 'They are a people whose hearts turn away from me. They refuse to do what I tell them.'

So in my anger I took an oath: 'They will never enter my place of rest.'"

"Bow Down and Worship Him," recorded by Bishop Paul S. Morton, is one of my favorite gospel songs that ushers me into the presence of the Holy Spirit. I grew up appreciating the various genres of gospel music. I learned at an early age the importance of praising and worshiping God, no matter the challenges or obstacles one may face. John 4:23-24 (NIV) states, "Yet a time is coming and has now come when the true worshipers will worship the Father in the Spirit and in truth, for they are the kind of worshipers the Father seeks. God is spirit, and his worshipers must worship in the Spirit and in truth."

Dr. Melva Wilson Costen, Professor Emeritus of Worship at The Interdenominational Theological Center (ITC) in Atlanta, Georgia, taught me that Christian worship is an acknowledgment of the response to the presence and power of God as revealed in Jesus Christ through the work of the Holy Spirit. She taught me that worship is the celebration of all that God has done, is doing, and will do in our lives. She instructed me that on Sunday mornings, God is the Center. Praying, singing, reading scripture, or the sermonic moment should build on one another. She taught me that the worship experience can be invigorated through our five senses. Dr. Costen believed that worship is a way to express our reverence and gratitude for God's grace and mercy, and to acknowledge God's sovereignty over all creation.

According to scholars, Psalms 95–99 are a compilation

of psalms that celebrate the theme of worship and emphasize God's power, holiness, and righteous judgment. Psalm 95 is interpreted as a Royal Psalm because it acknowledges God as "the great Creator and King," while also warning the reader against the hardening of hearts and disobeying God, drawing a similarity to the rebellious nature of the children of Israel in the wilderness. This psalm is linked with sabbath worship, and it has been sung as an invitation to worship in the Christian church.

Psalm 95:1-7a begins with a passionate call to praise God twice as the Creator and recognizes God as the "rock of our salvation." In addition, these verses emphasize God's sovereignty and highlight the relationship of shepherd and flock.

Psalm 95:7b-11 begins with the warning against disobedience, particularly at Meribah and Massah in the wilderness. In addition, these verses stress that God's children should learn from their past and respond to God with trust and obedience.

Prayer

O Lord, let us hear your voice and worship you with spirit and truth.

Amen.

Reflection

How do you describe a fervent worship experience?

Day 15 (Friday)

The Gift of Good Company

By Dr. Lewis E. Logan, II

Scripture:

Psalm 95

Collective Need for Salvation

We are reminded of our individual sins and the need for salvation, forgiveness, and deliverance. Yet, it is also crucial to recognize that this need also exists collectively. Jesus gave his life for all, and God's compassion extends to every human being. Together, we share the privilege and opportunity to come before God, not as isolated individuals, but as a gathered people.

The Strength of Community

Our spiritual journey is not one we undertake alone. There is power and encouragement in walking together—in good company. This "good company" moves in agreement with God, uniting in homage, thanksgiving, and appreciation. As God's people, our ultimate allegiance belongs to the Creator, and we are called to bow down and humble ourselves in God's presence, both with joy and gratitude.

Worship as Resistance and Distinction

Bowing before God is more than an act of humility—it is a declaration of resistance against the distractions and idols of our age. In a world filled with temptations—money, fame, comfort, and countless fleeting pursuits—true fulfillment is found only in relationship with God and in the fellowship of the faithful. The things we create or collect can never offer the deep joy or meaning that God alone provides.

Remembering Our Deliverance

When we bow to God, we reject the false gods of our culture and resist the lure of lesser allegiances—whether to power, nationality, or material success. We remember the God who delivers, just as the psalm recalls Israel's journey from bondage. Our deliverance is not merely an escape from hardship but an invitation into a journey with God, who continues to lead us forward.

Living in Good Company

Good company ties us both to God and to each other. We are created for community, to be God's people, the flock under God's care. Only the Creator deserves our ultimate commitment. Even our acts of worship become expressions of insistence, resistance, and self-determination—we bow to no one and nothing but God. We do not submit to political parties, personalities, nations, or systems that diminish others; our ultimate allegiance is to God alone.

Encouragement for the Journey

The good news is this: we are not alone. Others walk with us on this path. Let us continue the journey together, united in purpose and devotion.

Prayer

Lord, when I don't see how or when, please help me remember that I can always, always ask you. I promise to tell others what you have done and what I believe you will do!

Amen and Ase'.

Reflection

Can you ask and trust that God will make a way, especially when it seems impossible to you?

Day 16 (Saturday)

A Divine Encounter

By Bishop Sharma D. Lewis Logan

Scripture:

John 4:1-6 (CEB)

Jesus learned that the Pharisees had heard that he was making more disciples and baptizing more than John (although Jesus' disciples were baptizing, not Jesus himself). Therefore, he left Judea and went back to Galilee.

Jesus had to go through Samaria. He came to a Samaritan city called Sychar, which was near the land Jacob had given to his son Joseph. Jacob's well was there. Jesus was tired from his journey, so he sat down at the well. It was about noon.

Have you ever met a person who changed your life? Twelve years ago, I met my therapist, Dr. Lewis Kola, and in one sacred conversation, my life changed. I was forty-nine years old, and in a couple of months, I would be turning the big 5-0! Yes, the dreaded fifty.

When a few of my girlfriends turned fifty, something changed in their lives. There was an ongoing conversation about not being married or having children. There was constant conversation about approaching menopause because of balding, turning gray, and difficulties losing weight. I remember there was a continuous conversation on the effects of aging.

Interestingly, I found myself discussing my entire life with Dr. Kola. However, before we had the opportunity to dig into my life as a single, African American woman with no husband and no prospects, I was faced with the untimely death of three close relatives—my aunt, great-uncle, and my dad, who all shaped my life. My weekly sessions with Dr. Kola were critical, and he helped me unpack my life and face turning fifty. I have always felt that my meeting with Dr. Kola was not coincidental but a divine encounter ordained by God.

As described by *Merriam-Webster.com,* the word "encounter" means "to come upon face to face."[19] As we examine our text, there was a divine encounter between a Samaritan woman and Jesus. The Samaritan woman didn't have an encounter with just anyone; she had an encounter with our Savior, the chief cornerstone of our faith.

Have you ever had a personal encounter with the Lord? Where were you? Second Corinthians 5:17 (NIV) states, "Therefore, if anyone is in Christ, the new creation has come: The old has gone, the new is here!" The encounter with the Lord was the vehicle that changed the life of the Samaritan woman.

---

[19] *Merriam-Webster.com Dictionary,* s.v. "Encounter," accessed August 23, 2025, https://www.merriam-webster.com/dictionary/encounter.

In the text, Jesus encounters the Samaritan woman near the city of Sychar, approximately 1.5 kilometers from Jacob's well. At that time, Jews customarily avoided Samaria by traveling along the Jordan River. The Jewish people ostracized the Samaritans because they diverged from the Jewish faith.

Jesus, tired from his journey, sat down by the well and began to dialogue with the Samaritan woman. The divine encounter allows the reader to understand that even though the Master asked for water, he was the living water. In verse 10, Jesus answers, "If you knew the gift of God and who it is that asks you for a drink, you would have asked him, and he would have given you living water." According to *The Oxford Bible Commentary,* the theme of living water appears often in the Old Testament as an image of salvation, e.g., Isaiah 12:3, 55:1; Zechariah 14:8. Jesus, the Messiah, was determined to lead her to salvation, and no religious barrier was to circumvent this divine encounter. Jesus declared in John 6:35b (NIV), "And whoever believes in me will never be thirsty."

Prayer

O Lord, an unusual meeting can be a divine encounter.

Amen.

Reflection

Have you experienced a divine encounter that shaped your life?

Day 17 (Monday)

"Way Maker"

By Dr. Lewis E. Logan, II

Scripture:

Genesis 24:26-27 (NLT)

The man bowed low and worshiped the Lord. "Praise the Lord, the God of my master, Abraham," he said. "The Lord has shown unfailing love and faithfulness to my master, for he has led me straight to my master's relatives."

Personal Connection to the Song

One of my most cherished praise and worship songs is "Way Maker," which repeatedly declares God as a "way maker, miracle worker, promise keeper, and light in the darkness."[20] The lyrics resonate deeply with me, especially the verses that affirm God's ongoing presence and activity. The song speaks powerfully of God's nearness and attentiveness—God hears us because God is always present with us.

---

[20] Sinach,"Way Maker (Live)," YouTube video, 13:26, posted by Sinach, Dec 30, 2015, https://youtu.be/n4XWfwLHeLM and Leeland, "Way Maker," recorded 2019, track on *Better Word,* Integrity Music, streaming, Spotify.

Application to Challenging Times

This truth becomes especially meaningful when circumstances are unsettled and uncertain. Consider, for example, the experience of Eliezer, who was entrusted with the solemn duty of finding a wife for Isaac. Having been a long-time member of Abraham and Sarah's household, Eliezer witnessed their journey from struggle to trust and belief in God's promises. He understood the gravity of his responsibility—not only for Abraham's family but for the fulfillment of God's promise to them.

Faith and Trust in God the Way Maker

Eliezer's story teaches us about carrying the weight of destiny and the importance of trust. To be given such responsibility means recognizing our need for God's help. Eliezer models humility in his prayer: Lord, I don't know what I'm doing, but please help me navigate this challenging and unsettling season. We, too, are invited to pray with expectation and to praise God when our hope is fulfilled—knowing that God not only hears us but is actively helping us.

Participating in God's Way

God is our "Way Maker, promise keeper, and light in the darkness." God opens paths beyond what we can expect or imagine. We must be positioned where God can direct us so we are ready to witness the way God makes for us. In doing so, we align ourselves with God's guidance and provision. To God be the glory.

Prayer

You are the "way maker, miracle worker, promise keeper, and light in the darkness."

Amen and Ase'.

Watch the Original and Official Live rendition of Way Maker, written by Award Winning Song Writer, SINACH. The song has been translated to over 50 languages and covered by many artists all around the world:

youtu.be/QM8jQHE5AAk?si=wLfoZ_G9J963CSo_

Reflection

"Ask me and I will tell you remarkable secrets you do not know about things to come" (Jeremiah 33:3, NLT). *Just ask Me.*

Day 18 (Tuesday)

Obedience

By Bishop Sharma D. Lewis Logan

Scripture:

Psalm 81 (NRSVue)

Sing aloud to God our strength; shout for joy to the God of Jacob.
Raise a song; sound the tambourine, the sweet lyre with the harp.
Blow the trumpet at the new moon, at the full moon, on our festal day.
For it is a statute for Israel, an ordinance of the God of Jacob.
He made it a decree in Joseph, when he went out over[a] the land of Egypt.
I hear a voice I had not known:
"I relieved your shoulder of the burden; your hands were freed from the basket.
In distress you called, and I rescued you; I answered you in the secret place of thunder; I tested you at the waters of Meribah. Selah
Hear, O my people, while I admonish you; O Israel, if you would but listen to me!
There shall be no strange god among you; you shall not bow down to a foreign god.
I am the Lord your God, who brought you up out of the land of Egypt. Open your mouth wide, and I will fill it.

> *"But my people did not listen to my voice; Israel would not submit to me.*
> *So I gave them over to their stubborn hearts, to follow their own counsels.*
> *O that my people would listen to me, that Israel would walk in my ways!*
> *Then I would quickly subdue their enemies and turn my hand against their foes.*
> *Those who hate the Lord would cringe before him, and their doom would last forever.*
> *I would feed you[d] with the finest of the wheat, and with honey from the rock I would satisfy you."*

According to *The New Interpreter's Dictionary of the Bible*, "The word group *obey/disobey* occur 283 times in the Bible. However, when combined with related words that imply obedience the number increases to 6,302. Obedience is defined as a willing and active submission to God's will, commands, and authority."[21]

In today's text, scholars believe that Psalm 81 was perhaps written for the Feast of Tabernacles observed by the Israelites. This festival celebrated the forty-year wilderness journey. Psalm 81 reminds us to trust God's provision and not repeat Israel's faults. The Psalmist Asaph encourages Israel to worship God for delivering them from the Egyptians, to remember what God had done for them, and to repent for their ungratefulness. He also testified that if they obeyed God, God would bless

---

[21] *The New Interpreter's Dictionary of the Bible,* Katharine Doob Sakenfeld, vol. 2, ed. (Nashville: Abingdon Press, 2006–2009).

them with unexpected blessings. He reveals that if they do not listen, God will turn them over to their own evil desires.

Asaph begins in verses 1-2 by saying that everyone should praise God for God's power through singing, accompanied by the timbrel, harp, and lyre. He exhorts Israel that the law requires praise during the festival in verses 3-4.

"Praise" comes from a Latin word meaning "value" or "price." To give praise to God is to proclaim God's merit or God's worth. Praise is one of humanity's many responses to God's revelation of God's self. Praise is an act of worship, and our praise towards God is how we express our love and joy to the Lord.

In verses 5-6, the psalmist encourages the Israelites to remember that God brought them out of Egypt, set them free from bondage, and relieved their burden. In verse 7, he reminds them that God answered them out of a thundercloud and tested them at the waters of Meribah. Finally, Asaph invites the Israelites to listen to and obey God; as a result, their lives will be filled with blessings, their mouths filled with good things, and their enemies will be crushed. However, if they do not listen, Asaph shares in verses 8-16 that God will turn their rebellious attitudes over to their own evil desires.

Prayer

O Lord, let me be obedient to your will for my life. Amen.

Reflection

What lessons can we learn from the Israelites' mistakes?

Day 19 (Wednesday)

Spoiler Alert

By Dr. Lewis E. Logan, II

Scripture:

John 7:37-39 (NLT)

On the last day, the climax of the festival, Jesus stood and shouted to the crowds, "Anyone who is thirsty may come to me! Anyone who believes in me may come and drink! For the Scriptures declare, 'Rivers of living water will flow from his heart.'" (When he said "living water," he was speaking of the Spirit, who would be given to everyone believing in him. But the Spirit had not yet been given, because Jesus had not yet entered into his glory.)

Anticipation and Revelation

As a movie enthusiast, I have always found it fascinating how fellow fans and self-proclaimed experts strive to uncover the plot of a film before its release. They dissect trailers, analyze scenes, and speculate about the creator's intentions, hoping to predict how the story will unfold and whether it will measure up to others in its genre. Sometimes, people claim to have secret insights or exclusive knowledge about upcoming movies.

This sense of anticipation and search for hidden

meaning is echoed in John's narrative. In the wilderness season—a period between penitence and ministry—John, the Elder, offers us a revealing glimpse of Jesus. Much like a "spoiler alert," John's account gives us privileged knowledge about what is to come.

The Living Water Revealed

On the last day of the festival, Jesus stands as the embodiment of the Exodus narrative, yet updated in the present. He announces himself as the Living Water, the one who will bring forth the Holy Spirit. John's words are both a revelation and a preview, reminding us that Jesus is not only the source of spiritual sustenance but also the announcer of its arrival.

As we journey through this Lenten season towards transformational discipleship, it is vital to remember that, in moments when we feel weary or depleted, Jesus, the Living Water, is present to revive and sustain us. The Holy Spirit, promised by Jesus, flows abundantly to support and sustenance amidst parched realities (Exodus 17:6-7) in every desert place (Isaiah 43:19).

Courage and Humanity in the Face of Danger

John's spoiler alert also uncovers the courage of Jesus, who faces imminent threat and danger—there are those who wish to arrest him. Despite this, Jesus remains fully human, crying out and declaring his role as the source of Living Water. He is not a distant spirit but a tangible presence, blending metaphor and reality.

In the Festival of Sukkot (Tabernacles), amid wilderness and uncertainty, Jesus is the resource we need now and in the future. The spoiler alert is this: we have insider knowledge of Jesus' presence.

Jesus as the Rock and Living Water

Even when we feel besieged or endangered, Jesus sustains us. Physical water may be limited, but Jesus likens himself to the rock from which water flowed in the wilderness—a dual image that anchors and refreshes. He is the rock in a season of contention, surrounded by questions, anger, and tension. Yet, upon this rock, the church is built, and from him flows Living Water.

John's narrative is rich with layered meaning, offering both disclosure and double-speak—a revelation that Jesus is both the Living Water and the rock from which our spiritual life springs.

Prayer

Thank you, Lord, for urging me forward to the new things you are doing in me right now! Thank you for this refreshing season of fellowship that has already begun. I see it, I feel it, I know it, right now. It's like clarity amidst the noise and distraction and cool thirst-quenching waters flowing in arid dry spaces.

Amen and Ase.'

Reflection

Remember that commercial tag line, "Obey your thirst"? Hint: Sprite Spirit!

Day 20 (Thursday)

Words

By Bishop Sharma D. Lewis Logan

Scripture:

Ephesians 4:29 (NRSVue)

Do not let any unwholesome talk come out of your mouths, but only what is helpful for building others up according to their needs, that it may benefit those who listen.

In my neighborhood, we would often hear kids say to one another, "Sticks and stones may break my bones, but words will never hurt me." It is stated that words are essential because they serve as the building blocks for communication, influencing thoughts, actions, and relationships.

I have witnessed over the years how spoken words have impacted relationships, hurt feelings, and even caused physical altercations. How many times have we heard of individuals who have written or spoken inappropriate words about another person's race, culture, or sexual orientation? How many times have you drafted an email that you wished you had never clicked "send?" How many times have you received a letter that surprised you with the content written about you?

My husband reminds me often that words have "life and power." The words we utter every day have the power to build up or tear down, and we must never underestimate the power of words. The words we speak can encourage others, yet in the same sentence, they can discourage.

Amy Agarwal, principal writer for *EngenderHealth*, states, "The words we choose and the language we use have the power to affect the people and the world around us. Our words represent our beliefs, morals, prejudices, and principles—sometimes in ways we may not mean."[22]

Research in parenting and education suggests that children may hear as many as eighteen negative statements for every one positive one—a ratio often cited in classroom management literature.[23] According to Gallup, only one in three U.S. employees strongly agree they received recognition for good work in the past week, implying that roughly two-thirds experienced little to no recognition in that timeframe. Over a longer period, surveys suggest that about 40 percent of workers receive recognition only a few times a year or less.[24]

---

[22] Amy Agarwal, *EngenderHealth,* accessed August 28, 2025, https://www.engenderhealth.org.

[23] Commonly cited in classroom management research; see, for example, Jane Bluestein, *The Win-Win Classroom* (Thousand Oaks, CA: Corwin Press, 2010), 24.

[24] Gallup, "Employee Retention Depends on Getting Recognition Right," *Gallup Workplace,* January 17, 2024, https://www.gallup.com/workplace/650174/employee-retention-depends-getting-recognition-right.aspx; "Employee Recognition Statistics You Should Know in 2025," *High5 Test,* accessed August 12, 2025, https://high5test.com/employee-recognition-statistics/.

The Bible cautions us on how we use our words and, ultimately, how we use our tongues:

> *"The tongue has the power of life and death, and those who love it will eat its fruit."*
> **Proverbs 18:21 (NIV)**

> *"But no human being can tame the tongue. It is a restless evil, full of deadly poison."*
> **James 3:8 (NIV)**

> *"The words of the mouth are deep waters, but the fountain of wisdom is a rushing stream."*
> **Proverbs 18:4 (NIV)**

The reflection for today admonishes us, "Do not let any unwholesome talk [or foul language, NLT] come out of your mouths." Instead, the text instructs us to only speak "what is helpful for building others up according to their needs, that it may benefit those who listen" Ephesians 4:29 (NIV).

Prayer

O Lord, help me to recognize that words have meaning and power!

Amen.

Reflection

Have you ever spoken or written inappropriate words?

How did you rectify your mistake?

Day 21 (Friday)

Don't Act Your Age

By Dr. Lewis E. Logan, II

Scripture:

Ephesians 5:4-5 (NLT)

Obscene stories, foolish talk, and coarse jokes—these are not for you. Instead, let there be thankfulness to God. You can be sure that no immoral, impure, or greedy person will inherit the Kingdom of Christ and of God. For a greedy person is an idolater, worshiping the things of this world.

Understanding Spiritual Maturity Beyond Age

Many times, we are told to behave according to the expectations associated with our chronological age. This social norm sets standards for how people of different ages should act—children are given more latitude, while adults are held to more stringent standards. These expectations are influenced by the broader cultural context, the *sitz in leben,* and the age itself.

This was true in the time of the Apostle Paul, who offered guidance to Timothy, pastor of the church in Ephesus. In his letter, Paul instructed the community to avoid behaviors reflective of the prevailing ethos of their society. Rather than mirroring the culture around them, they were called to live out distinct and unique values. This included their language, attitudes, and overall conduct.

Ephesus was a thriving economic hub with its harbor, seacoasts, hills, fertile valleys, intersecting trade routes, and eclectic culture, much like Corinth. As a protectorate of the Roman Empire, it was marked by affluence and permissiveness. The church in Ephesus, meeting in homes and developing as a faith community, was continually challenged by the temptation to adopt the behaviors of its contemporaries. Paul's message called them to resist the influences of their "age."

While space may not permit a detailed reading here, Paul's counsel was clear: those who follow Christ are to act in accordance with their calling as disciples, not according to the shifting morals of their era. This encouragement is echoed in other scripture, such as 1 Corinthians 16:9, where Paul speaks of the tremendous opportunity for ministry in Ephesus.

The challenge remains relevant: we are not told to act as if our age is different, but rather to be discerning and wise. We must reject the lure to adopt the behaviors of those who do not share our hope, fellowship, or relationship with Jesus Christ and the power of the Holy Spirit. Discipleship may cost us friendships or relationships, but it calls us to be distinct and peculiar people.

With this in mind, our prayer is as simple as, "Lord, help me be a witness for you, no matter who is around me. May

I not reflect the morals of this age, but instead, embody the timeless values of your kingdom. In Jesus' name, Amen."

This message renews the call in Romans 12 to not be conformed to this world, but be transformed by the renewing of our minds, and the reminder to be "in the world but not of the world." The pull and distraction of culture are powerful, just as Jesus experienced temptation in the wilderness. Yet, we are called to be distinct people, strengthened in our resolve by the power of the Holy Spirit. In Jesus' name, Amen.

Prayer

"Prone to wander, Lord, I feel it, prone to leave the God I love ... Here's my heart, Lord, take and seal it, seal it for Thy courts above."[25]

Amen and Ase'.

Reflection

Augustine the African Bishop of Antiquity, wrote, "Lord, make me chaste, but not yet."[26]

---

[25] Robert Robinson, "Come, Thou Fount of Every Blessing," 1758; in *The African Methodist Episcopal Hymnal* (Nashville: African Methodist Episcopal Church, 2011), no. 77; and *The United Methodist Hymnal* (Nashville: United Methodist Publishing House, 1989), no. 400.

[26] Augustine of Hippo, *Confessions, Book VIII*, Henry Chadwick, trans. (Oxford: Oxford University Press, 1991), 152.

Day 22 (Saturday)

The Shepherd

By Bishop Sharma D. Lewis Logan

Scripture:

Psalm 23 (NKJV)

The Lord is my shepherd;
I shall not want.
He makes me to lie down in green pastures;
He leads me beside the still waters.
He restores my soul;
He leads me in the paths of righteousness
For His name's sake.

Yea, though I walk through the valley of the shadow
of death,
I will fear no evil;
For You are with me;
Your rod and Your staff, they comfort me.

You prepare a table before me in the presence of my
enemies;
You anoint my head with oil;
My cup runs over.
Surely goodness and mercy shall follow me
All the days of my life;
And I will dwell in the house of the Lord
Forever.

I remember learning The Twenty-Third Psalm as a child at home and in Sunday school at Brannen Chapel United Methodist Church in Statesboro, Georgia. My teacher, Mrs. Amanda Smith, would reward us with candy, games, and puzzles if we memorized and recited Bible verses. She would remind us that our spiritual food was the Word of God, and she would constantly quiz us on it. I always felt I had an advantage because on Saturdays, my mother would let me visit Mrs. Smith to help her prepare the Sunday school lessons.

The Twenty-Third Psalm was easy to memorize because I quickly recognized that the Psalmist David was describing God's loving care as a shepherd. Authored by David, this psalm is thought by scholars to reflect his life experiences. Some believe this psalm was written when David was king and needed God's protection, while others believe it was written when David was sent into the wilderness and escaped from the hands of Absalom.

This psalm is likened by all denominations. It brings hope and comfort to God's people and is often used during funeral services. If you need a scripture to reassure you of God as the shepherd, provider, protector, and guide, this text encompasses all these traits.

The psalm's main theme focuses on the relationship between God, the shepherd, and God's people, who are metaphorically compared to sheep in need of protection and guidance.

There are six key meanings within this text:

God as the Shepherd:

The Psalmist David uses the image of a shepherd to exemplify God's role in protecting, leading, and providing for God's people.

Provision:

Psalm 23:1, in the Amplified Bible Translation—"The Lord is my Shepherd, I shall not lack anything"—emphasizes God's provision of everything needed in life.

Guidance and Protection:

David stresses that the shepherd will lead his people to green pastures and still waters and will guide them through the valley of the shadow of death, signifying life's challenges.

God's Presence:

David underscores in the text that God's presence is always with God's people.

Comfort and Safety:

In the face of fear, David uses the image of the shepherd's rod and staff that brings guidance, protection, comfort, and safety.

Eternal Hope:

In the final verses, David expresses the hope for the future and the everlasting life that God will never leave us.

Prayer

O Lord, though I walk through the valley of the shadow of death, you are with me.

Amen.

Reflection

When did you learn The Twenty-Third Psalm? How do you apply Psalm 23 to your life?

Day 23 (Monday)

Transformational Experiences

By Dr. Lewis E. Logan, II

Scripture:

Acts 9:13-16 (NLT)

"But Lord," exclaimed Ananias, "I've heard many people talk about the terrible things this man has done to the believers in Jerusalem! And he is authorized by the leading priests to arrest everyone who calls upon your name."

But the Lord said, "Go, for Saul is my chosen instrument to take my message to the Gentiles and to kings, as well as to the people of Israel. And I will show him how much he must suffer for my name's sake."

A Personal Reflection on Grace

Transformational experiences are profound and life-altering. There was a time in my life when I refused to sing one of the most well-known hymns in all of Christendom—"Amazing Grace." I was deeply troubled after learning that its lyricist, John Newton, was once an unrepentant human trafficker, complicit in the suffering of countless African people and families. His particular cruelty extended to rape and abuse, especially towards young African girls and women.

The Lyricist's Journey

My perspective shifted when I learned about the lyricist's own transformational experience when he endured a near-death encounter at sea. As he attempted to climb above deck to escape drowning, a massive wave swept away a close fellow sailor right before his eyes. In that moment, his own mortality collided with the full weight of his past actions—the cries of innocent victims, the violence he inflicted, the destruction of families. Newton realized his life needed to change and that this might be his only opportunity for redemption.

Following this harrowing journey, John Newton began the grueling process of transformation, eventually becoming a minister, lyricist, and outspoken abolitionist. His life-changing experience inspired the words of "Amazing Grace," a hymn that continues to inspire redemptive hope and change for all. Newton, once a human trafficker, became a powerful voice against slavery. His transformation serves as a testament to the possibility of change in even the most sinful circumstances.

Understanding Ananias' Reluctance

With this story in mind, I can understand why Ananias was hesitant to obey God's command in Acts 9:13-16. Ananias was to go to Straight Street and lay hands on Saul, a notorious persecutor of Christians, murderer, blasphemer, and assassin. Despite his objections, God assured him that this individual had undergone a transformative change and would continue to transform as he fulfilled God's purposes. It could be said that both Saul and Ananias were blind. Saul was blinded by ambition to persecute Christians, and Ananias was blinded by the perception that Jesus could not redeem someone so wicked as Saul.

What a powerful example of amazing grace—a transformational experience that completely changed Saul, turning him from a persecutor of Jesus into the Apostle Paul.

Embracing God's Transformative Power

Like Ananias, I, too, grappled with the reality that God can use anyone, regardless of their past. This realization was itself a transformational experience for me, affirming that nothing can separate us from the love of God, as Paul later declares in Romans 8:38 (NLT):

> *And I am convinced that nothing can ever separate us from God's love. Neither death nor life, neither angels nor demons, neither our fears for today nor our worries about tomorrow—not even the powers of hell can separate us from God's love.*

These stories of change invite us to reflect on the power of grace—grace that reshapes lives and redirects destinies. They serve as reminders that no one is beyond redemption and that profound change is possible for all.

Reflecting on the origins of the songs and scriptures we cherish can deepen our understanding of the human condition. Each encounter with these sacred words is an invitation to remember the possibility of new beginnings and the enduring hope of transformation.

A Hope for the Journey

Transformational experiences are not confined to the past; they remain possible for each of us today. As I continue this Lenten journey and anticipate seasons yet to come, I look forward to further transformational experiences.

Prayer

Lord, I pray that you forgive me for the people I've hurt and the harm that I have done. Help me to forgive myself. Lord, I come just as I am.

Amen and Ase'.

Reflection

Listen to William McDowell sing, "I give myself away, so You can use me"[27] online at:

youtu.be/ZweMABLgluY?si=CQg2h85lVdsjtQiq

Reflect on the words in the hymn "Amazing Grace": "I once was lost, but now am found, Was blind, but now I see."

---

[27] William McDowell, "I Give Myself Away (Live)," YouTube video, 11:11, October 22, 2009.

Day 24 (Tuesday)

"Praise Is What I Do!"

By Bishop Sharma D. Lewis Logan

Scripture:

Psalm 146 (CEB)

Praise the Lord!
Let my whole being[a] praise the Lord!
I will praise the Lord with all my life; I will sing praises to my God as long as I live.
Don't trust leaders; don't trust any human beings— there's no saving help with them!
Their breath leaves them, then they go back to the ground. On that very same day, their plans die too.
The person whose help is the God of Jacob— the person whose hope rests on the Lord their God— is truly happy!
God: the maker of heaven and earth, the sea, and all that is in them, God: who is faithful forever,
who gives justice to people who are oppressed, who gives bread to people who are starving!
The Lord: who frees prisoners.
The Lord: who makes the blind see. The Lord: who straightens up those who are bent low. The Lord: who loves the righteous.
The Lord: who protects immigrants, who helps orphans and widows, but who makes the way of the wicked twist and turn!
The Lord will rule forever! Zion, your God will rule from one generation to the next!
Praise the Lord!

In 2005, the hit gospel song on all radio stations was Bishop William Murphy's "Praise Is What I Do." You could not turn on the radio or attend an African American church without hearing this song being played or sung on Sunday mornings. The lyrics express a life of continual worship and devotion and proclaim that praise is not just an action but an identity ("praise is who I am").[28]

According to the *New Interpreter's Dictionary* of the Bible, "Praise is defined as the human activity, oriented toward others in a gesture of gratitude and exaltation for the person, accomplishments, and presence of others." The definition further clarifies that "the unsolicited and unmerited character of praise brings joy, satisfaction, and builds bonds between those praised and the one who offers praise.[29]

The most common Hebrew words for "praise" are *hala* (verb) and *tehillah* (noun). And the most persistent call to praise appears in Psalm 150, where the form of these words appears thirteen times in six verses. In the Old and New Testaments, praise is primarily directed toward God and is an act of worship.

As we reflect on today's passage of Scripture, found in Psalm 146, the psalmist encourages the people to praise and trust the Lord. Psalm 146, usually described as a

---

[28] William Murphy, "Praise Is What I Do," Kingdom Records, 2002.

[29] The New Interpreter's Dictionary of the Bible, s.v. "Praise."

hymn of praise, is the first of the five psalms known as the Hallelujah Psalms. The psalmist focuses the reader on God's nature in verses 5-6 and God's actions in verses 6-9.

According to scholars, the basis for trusting God is God's dependability and humanity's fallibility. Psalm 146, in verses 1-2, begins and ends with a declaration to "Praise the Lord." The psalmist in verses 3-4 warns the reader against depending upon human beings, who cannot save. In verses 6-9, the psalmist describes God as a promise keeper, upholding the oppressed, feeding the hungry, freeing the prisoners, giving sight to the blind, protecting foreigners, and caring for orphans and widows. Finally, in verse 10, the psalmist speaks of God as being eternal.

Prayer

"O Lord, praise is what I do when I wanna be close to you."

Amen.

Reflection

What motivates you to praise God?

Day 25 (Wednesday)

Title: Isness and Oughtness

By Dr. Lewis E. Logan, II

Scripture:

Psalm 146

As I engage with Psalm 146, I am struck by the perspective of the psalmist. Could it be that the challenges and injustices observed in our current times were also present in the psalmist's day? The psalmist's context may have been under the crushing weight of empires like Assyria, Babylonia, or Persia, and yet, the response remains a resounding "Hallelujah."

Today, though I may not live under foreign occupation, I exist in within structures of an empire and see injustices and inhumanity inflicted on the powerless around the world: endless wars, mass incarceration and deportation, indiscriminate violence, injustice, genocides, weaponized rape, war profiteering, governmental and judicial corruption, blatant secular and religious bigotry, lgbtqia persecution, fascism, ethnic profiling, economic and environmental injustice, and massive refugee displacement and exploitation are among many deeply troubling existential realities. Scapegoating undocumented individuals fleeing hardship and oppression in their native communities, often as a result of global policies, is ever-present.

And yet, there is a kind of genius in defiantly proclaiming "Hallelujah"—a refusal to let the *isness* of this current age gag gladness and extinguish hope in imminent "oughtness." This song of praise becomes not just resistance but a reimagining of what ought to be or even will be: a future shaped by justice and compassion.

Believing, therefore, is never enough. Ultimately, believing is becoming and "oughtness" is "isness." We are reminded that the Creator of this earth sees both the beauty and the devastation—polluted lands and renewed habitats, overexploited resources and cultivated bio-diversities, and the suffering of those cast aside and those stepping up. Trusting God means believing, alongside the psalmist, that justice will come for the oppressed, food for the hungry, and freedom for those disappeared, deported, or incarcerated for and through them. Believing, therefore, is never enough. Ultimately, believing is becoming. *Oughtness* will become *isness*.

The rhetorical tension is implicit in the psalmist's query: "How do you sing the Lord's song in a strange land?" (Psalm 137:4, KJV). How can we offer a "Hallelujah" for an *oughtness* when our *isness* is a hell reality so far from what ought to be?

We are called to pray, persevere, and continue the

song—even when it is a song of longing and resistance. Let us press on, family, facing the is forward while embracing the struggles for *ought*.

Prayer

"May your Kingdom come soon. May your will be done on earth, as it is in heaven. Give us today the food we need, and forgive us our sins, as we have forgiven those who sin against us. And don't let us yield to temptation, but rescue us from the evil one" (Matthew 6:10-13, NLT).

Amen and Ase'.

Reflection

"The arc of the universe is long, but it bends towards justice."[30]

---

[30] Theodore Parker, *Ten Sermons of Religion* (Boston: Crosby, Nichols, and Company, 1853), 84. Quoted and popularized by Martin Luther King, Jr., in speeches including "Remaining Awake Through a Great Revolution," National Cathedral, Washington, DC, March 31, 1968.

Day 26 (Thursday)

The Angel and the Scroll

By Bishop Sharma D. Lewis Logan

Scripture:

Revelation 10:1-11 (CEB)

Then I saw another powerful angel coming down from heaven. He was robed with a cloud, with a rainbow over his head. His face was like the sun, and his feet were like fiery pillars. He held an open scroll in his hand. He put his right foot on the sea and his left foot on the land. He called out with a loud voice like a lion roaring, and when he called out, the seven thunders raised their voices. When the seven thunders spoke, I was about to write, but I heard a voice from heaven say, "Seal up what the seven thunders have said, and don't write it down."

Then the angel I saw standing on the sea and on the land raised his right hand to heaven. He swore by the one who lives forever and always, who created heaven and what is in it, the earth and what is in it, and the sea and what is in it, and said, "The time is up. In the days when the seventh angel blows his trumpet, God's mysterious purpose will be accomplished, fulfilling the good news he gave to his servants the prophets."

Then the voice I heard from heaven spoke to me again and said, "Go, take the opened scroll from the hand of the angel who stands on the sea and on the land." So I went to the angel and told him to give me the scroll. He said to me, "Take it and eat it. It will make you sick to your stomach, but sweet as honey in your mouth." So I took the scroll from the angel's hand and ate it. And it was sweet as honey in my mouth, but when I swallowed it, it made my stomach churn. I was told, "You must prophesy again about many peoples, nations, languages, and kings."

The Book of Revelation has always been an intriguing book to read, especially in trying to understand its symbols, metaphors, and themes. It reveals current and future events and offers hope to believers that evil will be ultimately defeated, and we will gain eternal life with Jesus Christ. Revelation teaches us that Christ will return, evil will be conquered, and the dead will receive eternal life or eternal damnation.

Today's text describes a vision of a mighty angel who is to announce the final judgments on the earth. According to scholars, the angel's appearance with a rainbow, cloud, and fire-like feet denotes the divine presence, authority, and judgment.

The text begins with the angel holding a scroll in his hand, and he stands on the land and sea in verse 2. Scholars believe the angel's posture on both the land and sea characterizes the dominion over all creation. The text shifts, and John hears the seven thunders but is forbidden to write it down in verses 3-4, signifying the power and judgment of God. In verses 5-7, the angel shares that God's message will be revealed at the sound of the seventh trumpet.

The mission given to John is to eat the scroll held by the angel. The scroll will taste like honey in his mouth and will turn sour in his stomach. This is interpreted as a divine mission to proclaim God's Word, with the taste of honey representing the joy of the message and the sorrow representing the consequences of sin and judgments in verses 8-10. Finally, in verse 11, John will prophesy again by writing about the concerns of nations, tribes, and kings, and indicate the need for believers to internalize and declare God's message.

Prayer

"O taste and see that the Lord is good; blessed is the one who takes refuge in him" (Psalm 34:8, KJV).

Amen.

Reflection

What does it mean to "eat" the little book?

Day 27 (Friday)

Focused!

By Dr. Lewis E. Logan, II

Scripture:

Psalm 130:5-6 (NLT)

I am counting on the LORD; yes, I am counting on him. I have put my hope in his word. I long for the Lord more than sentries long for the dawn, yes, more than sentries long for the dawn.

The Pilgrims' Journey

Pilgrims from every corner of Palestine ascend the steep hill to Jerusalem, gathering for sacred celebrations. Some begin their journey from the depths of places like Jericho and Bethany, climbing nearly 3,000 feet to reach the city, which itself stands 2,400 feet above sea level. The path is challenging and demanding, with many undertaking this trek three times a year, as prescribed in Leviticus 23, for occasions such as Passover and Pentecost.

A Community United

This journey is more than a solitary climb; it is a communal effort. Singing is not only a way to pass the time but also becomes a shared act of encouragement, helping pilgrims focus and struggle together. By joining voices, they foster unity and strengthen their resolve to reach the presence of the Lord.

Determination and Purpose

The pilgrims' focus is unwavering, centered on one God, one goal, and the shared hope of connection with the divine. The songs and the journey itself reinforce their determination, reminding them that this ascent is not taken alone. Together, they rise to new heights of awareness and purpose, seeking the assurance that each day brings something new, a dawning of hope and fresh opportunities.

Gratitude for Blessings

The journey is marked by gratitude and thanksgiving, especially during the harvest season. Pilgrims remember that all they have comes from the Lord, making the experience intentional, purposeful, and deeply meaningful.

Unity and Expectation

Walking together as a community, the pilgrims anticipate a great gathering in the Promised Land. Their regular assembly is powerful, as it connects their history and destiny. This collective expectation fills them with joy, embodying the true benefit of remaining focused: staying the course and pressing toward what lies ahead.

Stay the course! There is far more ahead than behind.

Prayer

Lord, please help me/us to be strong and immovable—always working enthusiastically for you, knowing that all that we do for you, Lord, makes a difference.

Amen and Ase'.

Reflection

"I don't believe He brought me/us this far to leave me/us."[31]

---

[31] Curtis Burrell, "I Don't Feel No Ways Tired," recorded by James Cleveland and the Charles Fold Singers, James Cleveland and the Charles Fold Singers Live in Cincinnati, Savoy Records, 1978, LP.

Day 28 (Saturday)

Hope in the Midst of Hardship

By Bishop Sharma D. Lewis Logan

Scripture:

Psalm 130 (NRSVue)

Out of the depths I cry to you, O Lord.
Lord, hear my voice!
Let your ears be attentive to the voice of my supplications!
If you, O Lord, should mark iniquities, Lord, who could stand?
But there is forgiveness with you, so that you may be revered.
I wait for the Lord; my soul waits, and in his word I hope; my soul waits for the Lord more than those who watch for the morning, more than those who watch for the morning.
O Israel, hope in the Lord! For with the Lord there is steadfast love, and with him is great power to redeem.
It is he who will redeem Israel from all its iniquities.

Google describes "hardship" as "severe suffering."[32] Hardship can come in many forms, including illness, change of employment, loss of income, natural disasters, and divorce.

"Hope," as described by *Nelson's New Illustrated Bible*

---

[32] Oxford Languages, *Oxford English Dictionary* via Google, s.v. "Hardship," accessed August 25, 2025, https://www.google.com.

Dictionary, is "looking forward with confidence to a future good."[33] The Bible has a great deal to say about hope. Hope does not arise from an individual's desires but from God, who is the believer's hope. Genuine hope is not merely ambitious thinking but a firm assurance about things that are both seen and unseen.

The Bible states that when we have "faith in Christ," we have hope for things eternal, things that will never decay or waste away. There will be circumstances in our lives when we experience suffering, pain, and hardship, as the Apostle Paul reminds us, "Because we know that suffering produces perseverance; perseverance, character; and character, hope" (Romans 5:3-4, NIV). During hardship, we should look to God not only to give us strength but to give us patience and the ability to endure. Evangelist Billy Graham once said, "The world today desperately hungers for hope, and yet uncounted people have almost given up" (Billy Graham Evangelistic Association).

C.S. Lewis once stated that hope is one of the theological virtues and something that a Christian is meant to do. We have hope in Jesus Christ, which means we can approach any hardship or suffering with vigor and strength.

Psalm 130 is one of the Penitential Psalms, a call for help, a cry for forgiveness, and a call to wait for the Lord in hope.

Those who wait on the Lord wait in hope. The psalmists

---

[33] *Nelson's New Illustrated Bible Dictionary,* s.v. "Hope."

tell us three things about waiting on the Lord. First, we must cry to the Lord for mercy. Secondly, wait for the Lord expectantly, and finally, we put our hope in the Lord.

As we examine the text, the psalmist writes in verses 1-4 that he is in a "low and deep place, crying to the Lord." Look at verses 1-2, "Out of the depths I cry to you; O Lord. O Lord, hear my voice. Let your ears be attentive to my cry for mercy." Scholars believe "the low place" represents when you hit rock bottom, and you realize you can't fix life on your own. As we examine the text in verses 5-6, the psalmist indicates we wait for the Lord expectantly.

"Hope," defined in *Nelson's New Illustrated Bible Dictionary,* means "confident expectancy."[34] In these two verses, the psalmist repeats five times that his hope is in the Lord. This was a confident expectation in God, who is always faithful to God's promise. I have come to realize in life that I do not base hope on my temporary feelings or circumstances. I base my hope on the Word of God and trust God's promises that are revealed in Scripture. Trust is the confidence in the character of God.

Finally, as we wait, we must put our hope in the Lord. This psalm moves from the experience of an individual to that of the community. According to the text, in verses 7-8, "for with the Lord is unfailing love," and the Lord will redeem God's people from their sins.

---

[34] *Nelson's New Illustrated Bible Dictionary,* s.v. "Hope."

Prayer

O Lord, my hope is in you. Amen.

Reflection

In the midst of handling obstacles, how do you maintain your hope in the Lord?

Day 29 (Monday)

Shut Up by Shame

By Dr. Lewis E. Logan, II

Scripture:

Psalm 51:15 (NLT)

Unseal my lips, O Lord, that my mouth may praise you.

Reflection on David's Journey

Samuel offers a look back at David's life, illustrating how admiration and curiosity led to a tragic chain of events, marked by severe suffering and devastating loss. Though it may be easy to judge David by his worst actions, it's important to remember he was not only the cherished psalmist and brave warrior but also someone whose story included grave errors—David, the rapist, the murderer, the conspirator, and yet also David, the man after God's own heart. These moments are not the sum total of his life—nor do any singular actions define us completely. We are similar to David; it is not enough to merely condemn him. His story reminds us that we are all a complex blend of strengths and shortcomings.

We are also reminded of how absolute power corrupts

absolutely, as David the Monarch brazenly used his power and position to rape, scheme, lie, murder at will, and attempt to obstruct justice. In essence, David symbolizes the potential of powerful people and nations to traffic in unspeakable brutalities. Ironically, and perhaps fortunately, these complex contradictions are mitigated by the same courageous push past catastrophic lockjaw.

The Importance of Confession and Renewal

David's true greatness lies not only in his triumphs but in his willingness to repent, confess, and seek restoration, as he does in Psalm 51—a heartfelt plea for forgiveness. Verse 15, in particular, highlights the need to move beyond shame and disappointment, reaching out for God's compassion and mercy.

God knows every aspect of who we are—the good and the bad—and still loves us. This is why we must not let shame silence our voices. Even when darkness surrounds us, shame must not silence us. Life and death are in the power of our tongues.

The Power of Speaking Out

Proverbs teaches that the tongue holds the power of life and death. Even in our lowest contradictory moments, deliverance, repentance, forgiveness, and renewal are possible—if we are vulnerable, like David, to confess and brave enough, like Nathan, to confront. Are we not, at times, either or both? I can't hear you speak up!

An Illustration from *The Matrix*

A memorable example comes from the 1999 film *The Matrix*. Early in the story, before Neo knows his true identity, Agent Smith tries to silence him during an interrogation by sealing his mouth shut. Neo cannot speak, and fear overtakes him. Although he isn't physically restrained, the inability to speak is immediate and terrifying.[35] In the same way, shame can silence us and try to rob us of the breath of deliverance. We must refuse to be shut up by shame. Our deliverance lies in our willingness to speak up—always just a breath away.

Prayer

"May God grant us all the strength and courage to honor the dignity of every human being, to speak the truth to one another in love, and to walk humbly with one another and our God, for the good of all people of this nation and the world."[36]

Amen and Ase'.

Reflection

"First they came for the Communists, and I did not speak out—because I was not a Communist. Then they came for

---

[35] *The Matrix*, directed by Lana Wachowski and Lilly Wachowski (Burbank, CA: Warner Bros. Pictures, 1999), streaming, Netflix.

[36] Mariann Edgar Budde, "Service of Prayer for the Nation—Presidential Inauguration 2025" (Washington National Cathedral, January 21, 2025), YouTube video, 1:08:45, posted by "Washington National Cathedral," January 21, 2025, https://youtu.be/xwwaEuDeqM8.

the Socialists, and I did not speak out—because I was not a Socialist. Then they came for the trade unionists, and I did not speak out—because I was not a trade unionist. Then they came for the Jews, and I did not speak out—because I was not a Jew. Then they came for me—and there was no one left to speak out for me."[37]

---

[37] Martin Niemöller, remarks at the Confessing Church meeting, Frankfurt, Germany, 1946; quoted in They Thought They Were Free: The Germans, 1933–45, by Milton Mayer (Chicago: University of Chicago Press, 1955), 166.

Day 30 (Tuesday)

Save Me

By Bishop Sharma D. Lewis Logan

Scripture:

Psalm 143 (NIV)

Lord, hear my prayer, listen to my cry for mercy;
  in your faithfulness and righteousness come to my relief.
Do not bring your servant into judgment,
  for no one living is righteous before you.
The enemy pursues me, he crushes me to the ground;
  he makes me dwell in the darkness like those long dead.
So my spirit grows faint within me;
  my heart within me is dismayed.
I remember the days of long ago; I meditate on all your
  works and consider what your hands have done.
I spread out my hands to you;
  I thirst for you like a parched land.
Answer me quickly, Lord;
  my spirit fails.
Do not hide your face from me
  or I will be like those who go down to the pit.
Let the morning bring me word of your unfailing love,
  for I have put my trust in you.
Show me the way I should go,
  for to you I entrust my life.

> *Rescue me from my enemies, Lord,*
> *for I hide myself in you.*
>
> *Teach me to do your will, for you are my God;*
> *may your good Spirit lead me on level ground.*
>
> *For your name's sake, Lord, preserve my life;*
> *in your righteousness, bring me out of trouble.*
>
> *In your unfailing love, silence my enemies;*
> *destroy all my foes, for I am your servant.*

Just like the Psalmist David, I long for the time alone with God as I prepare to take my renewal leave. My renewal leave is used to rest, recharge, and re-imagine for the next ministry year. I travel to my second home and spend concentrated time in praying, reading God's Word, and reflecting upon the life of ministry.

As I examine the text for today, I can identify with the Psalmist David as he yearns for a time alone with God after feeling crushed by his enemies. I know you are probably reading and wondering, How does an episcopal leader feel crushed by the enemy? Let me count the ways: following *The Book of Discipline,* which, for some Methodists, feels obsolete now, leading an annual conference through the COVID-19 pandemic in 2020, where some people refused to wear a mask for their safety, and leading the annual conference through the dreaded "D word" called "disaffiliation."

As we open the text, David prays for God to save him. Crushed by his enemies, he prays for victory, deliverance, spiritual guidance, and revival. People often ask me what I enjoy about being a bishop. But rarely does anyone ask, Have you ever found yourself feeling alone and defeated?

Psalm 143 is described as one of the Penitential Psalms, where David confesses his sins and his desire to repent. This psalm reveals David's awareness of his own unrighteousness while pleading for God's grace and mercy. David was losing hope, caught in the paralyzing fear of depression.

Depression is real. For some individuals, it is so debilitating that it leads to death. Depression is described as a group of conditions associated with the elevation or lowering of a person's mood. As I continue in this work as an episcopal leader, I have become very sensitive to this medical illness, which can negatively affect how one feels, thinks, and performs the work of ministry.

Psychiatry.org reports, "Nearly three in ten adults (29%) have been diagnosed with depression at some point in their lives and about 18% are currently experiencing depression, according to a 2023 national survey."[38] Women are more likely than men, and younger adults are more likely than older adults to experience depression. If we are honest with ourselves, we can feel caught in depression and unable to pull ourselves out of

---

[38] American Psychiatric Association, "Nearly Three in Ten U.S. Adults Report Having Been Diagnosed with Depression," Psychiatry.org, May 3, 2023. https://www.psychiatry.org/news-room/news-releases/nearly-three-in-ten-u-s-adults-report-having-been-diagnosed-with-depression.

our situation. It is during these times that we can come to God and express our true feelings, knowing that God is our refuge and strength. In this text, David petitions God for five solutions to his problem:

- Save me because of your faithfulness and righteousness (verse 1).
- Save me because you previously saved others (verse 5).
- Save me because I reach out to you (verse 6).
- Save me because I run to hide in you (verse 9).
- Save me for your name's sake (verses 11-12).

Ultimately, Psalm 143 is a powerful expression of human weaknesses and dependence on God, marked by a deep longing for God's grace, mercy, guidance, and deliverance. I encourage anyone who is reading this devotion, if you feel you have slipped into a state of depression, please reach out to someone to share your feelings.

Prayer

"Lord, hear my prayer, listen to my cry for mercy; in your faithfulness and righteousness come to my relief" (Psalm 143:1, NIV).

Amen.

Reflection

In my human weakness, how do I cope with my feelings?

Day 31 (Wednesday)

Cardiac Bypass

By Dr. Lewis E. Logan, II

Scripture:

Jeremiah 39–41

Jeremiah's Fidelity and Courage

Jeremiah's unwavering faithfulness and courage as a prophet placed him in opposition to the ruling authorities during a time of siege. His life stands as a confirmation of the enduring power of God's Word, offering hope of restoration to the land, transformation of the heart, and a promise of renewal beyond captivity. Even in the face of judgment, God's assurance of future hope remains steadfast.

The Heart and Its Defects: A Metaphor

The human heart, both literally and metaphorically, is central to life. Medical conditions such as congenital heart defects—where four separate problems combine to disrupt the flow of blood—illustrate the delicacy, primacy, and vulnerability of the heart. In life-threatening conditions like "blue baby syndrome," restricted pulmonary arteries and septal defects prevent blood from circulating properly, turning the skin blue.

Something the Lord Made,[39] a 2004 movie starring Mos Def and Alan Rickman serves as both metaphor and miraculous methodology in the sense that the repair to the human heart requires divine intervention.

Innovation and Healing

Just as in *Something the Lord Made,* medical pioneers like Vivian Thomas and Dr. Alfred Blalock collaborated to address blue baby syndrome, so, too, does God act as the ultimate surgeon of our spiritual hearts. Through unprecedented procedures that once seemed impossible, they transformed the field of heart surgery. In the same way, God works in and through us, addressing the deformities and failures of the human heart.

The Heart as the Center of Life and Choice

In the biblical sense, the heart is more than just an organ; it is the seat of affection, thought, and free will. Here dwell our deepest devotions and the very freedom to choose. Jeremiah uses the metaphor of the heart to express the spiritual condition of the people, revealing both their need for healing and God's relentless commitment to redemption.

---

[39] https://en.wikipedia.org/wiki/Something_the_Lord_Made.

Transformation through Divine Intervention

God, as both Creator and Master Surgeon, is continually at work to redeem and restore relationships. Just as innovative medicine can bypass blockages and create new pathways for life, God unblocks the spiritual arteries of the heart, bringing vitality and power. Divine love, shown supremely through Jesus, can transform even the hardest heart, disobedience-clogged arteries of affection—replacing stony hearts with ones that beat anew in love and devotion.

The Promise of a New Heart

God's ultimate hope is that through divine cardiac intervention, a new thing will happen within us. The Creator is able to correct the congenital and restrictive deformations of the heart and mind, leading to true transformation. Through the power of unconditional love, God continues to work on us, in us, for us, and with us, bringing about spiritual healing and renewal.

Prayer

"Create in me a clean heart, O God. Renew a loyal spirit within me. Do not banish me from your presence, and don't take your Holy Spirit from me. Restore to me the joy of your salvation, and make me willing to obey you. Create in me a clean heart O God, renew a right Spirit within me" (Psalm 51:10-12, NLT).

Amen and Ase'.

Reflection

"Our God is a heart fixer and a mind regulator."[40]

---

[40] Traditional saying in African American preaching, often attributed to the "foremothers and forefathers of the faith."

Day 32 (Thursday)

When Believers Pray ...

By Bishop Sharma D. Lewis Logan

Scripture:

Philippians 1:1-11 (NIV)

Paul and Timothy, servants of Christ Jesus,

To all God's holy people in Christ Jesus at Philippi, together with the overseers and deacons:

Grace and peace to you from God our Father and the Lord Jesus Christ.

I thank my God every time I remember you. In all my prayers for all of you, I always pray with joy because of your partnership in the gospel from the first day until now, being confident of this, that he who began a good work in you will carry it on to completion until the day of Christ Jesus.

It is right for me to feel this way about all of you, since I have you in my heart and, whether I am in chains or defending and confirming the gospel, all of you share in God's grace with me. God can testify how I long for all of you with the affection of Christ Jesus.

And this is my prayer: that your love may abound more and more in knowledge and depth of insight, so that you may be able to discern what is best and may be pure and blameless for the day of Christ, filled with the fruit of righteousness that comes through Jesus Christ—to the glory and praise of God.

We live in a time where prayer is more crucial than ever. I've always believed and preached that prayer is one of the most underutilized spiritual disciplines in our churches and personal lives.

Prayer is so important to the life of a believer that it is mentioned more than 250 times in the scriptures. I believe that prayer has power over everything and is not an exercise in futility. Prayer is a powerful spiritual weapon and is essential to sustaining our faith. Jesus modeled a life of prayer in John 17, where he prayed for himself, the disciples, and all future believers.

Prayer is simply our communication with God. Prayer has been described as "too deep for words."

- John Wesley stated that "prayer is the grand means of drawing near to God."[41]
- Maya Angelou stated, "I know that when I pray, something wonderful happens. Not just to the person or persons for whom I'm praying, but also something wonderful happens to me."[42]
- Richard Foster stated, "To pray is to change. Prayer is the central avenue God uses to transform us."[43]
- Terry Teykl stated that "praying is connecting to God's heart."[44]

---

[41] John Wesley, "Sermon 21: Upon Our Lord's Sermon on the Mount, Discourse the Sixth," in The Works of John Wesley, 3rd ed. (Grand Rapids: Baker, 1979).

[42] Morgan Lee, "Seven Quotes Showing Maya Angelou's Love of the Bible and Faith," The Christian Post, May 28, 2014.

[43] Richard J. Foster, *Celebration of Discipline: The Path to Spiritual Growth* (San Francisco: HarperSanFrancisco, 1978).

[44] Terry Teykl, *The Chronicles of Prayer: A History of Prayer in the Christian Tradition, Praying in Jesus' Name for 21 Centuries* (Houston: Prayer Point Press, 2021).

- Martin Luther King stated that "to be a Christian without prayer is no more possible than to be alive without breathing."[45]
- Soren Kierkegaard stated, "The function of prayer is not to influence God, but rather to change the nature of the one who prays."[46]

I want to challenge you that if you are not praying by faith, it is counterproductive, and we typically pray according to our level of faith. When I pray, I utilize the scriptures because I've come to recognize that God responds to God's Word. The Bible declares:

- "The effectual fervent prayers of the righteous availeth much" (James 5:16, KJV).
- "By his wounds you have been healed" (1 Peter 2:24, ESV).
- "Do not be anxious about anything, but in everything by prayer and supplication with thanksgiving let your requests be made known to God" (Philippians 4:6, NASB).

Our prayers are falling to the ground because we are praying from an emotional space rather than a discerning one. When I pray, I ask God to give me the discernment in the Spirit to pray in agreement with God. First John 5:14-15 (NIV) reminds us, "This is the confidence we have in approaching God: that if we ask anything according to his will, he hears us. And if we

---

[45] Martin Luther King Jr., "The Power of Persistent Prayer," Strength to Love (New York: Harper & Row, 1963), 145.

[46] Søren Kierkegaard, Purity of Heart Is to Will One Thing, trans. Douglas V. Steere (New York: Harper & Brothers, 1938), 200.

know that he hears us—whatever we ask—we know that we have what we asked of him."

As the text opens, Paul is writing to the pastors, deacons, and all Christians in Philippi for whom he prays. He expresses his affection for the Philippian believers both in and out of prison as they have partnered to share and spread the gospel message. The text reveals that Paul prays for the Philippians to be filled with love and the fruits of righteousness, and that they might have the gift of discernment. Finally, he challenges the Philippians to live a life that is pleasing to God until the return of Jesus Christ.

Prayer

O Lord, give me the desire like Paul and Timothy to pray and walk the journey with others.

Amen.

Reflection

When believers pray, what happens?

_____

_____

_____

_____

Day 33 (Friday)

The Struggle Is Real

By Dr. Lewis E. Logan, II

Scripture:

Philippians 1:29-30 (NLT)

For you have been given not only the privilege of trusting in Christ but also the privilege of suffering for him. We are in this struggle together. You have seen my struggle in the past, and you know that I am still in the midst of it.

The Reality of the Struggle

Paul addresses the church in Philippi from house arrest, a situation he describes in terms of being "in chains," though these are not literal chains. While he is restricted in movement, he can still receive visitors and awaits a court hearing—likely the one around 60-64 AD—set in motion by his appeal to Caesar after a dramatic series of events.

Suffering for the Gospel

Paul's suffering is not accidental; it is the result of his commitment to serve Jesus and spread the gospel. The difficulties of his missionary journeys have led him to this point. He now endures both internal and external struggles inherent to his role as an apostle and witness for Christ. His journey is marked not by convenience but by sacrifice and challenge.

Internal and External Challenges

Paul's narrative reveals a tension between his deep desire to be in the presence of Jesus—whom he loves intimately—and his drive to continue ministering and sharing the gospel. He has learned to transform his captivity into opportunity, continuing his work even while constrained.

Yet, the struggle is more than internal. Some oppose the preaching of the gospel. Some go as far as to poison the judicial process and spread falsehoods about Paul's intentions and the work of the church.

Endurance in Faith

In this context, Paul offers a powerful perspective on sacrifice. He is fully invested and determined to persevere through every struggle, not as a temporary effort but as a lifelong commitment. This is not a "forty-day" process or a fleeting moment; it is a way of life.

Paul's experience serves as a gentle reminder for us, especially during this Lenten season. The struggle—whether it involves self-sacrifice, suffering for Christ, facing fears, or navigating personal challenges—is a daily reality for those who follow Jesus.

The Purpose of Struggle

Struggle, Paul suggests, is not senseless. It is a means, not an end—a process through which we are perfected. Through selfless service and the work of the Holy Spirit, our struggles are transformed for the sake of Christ and the good of humanity. The struggle is real, both within and without, but it is also purposeful and redemptive.

Prayer

My Comforter, I ask for your strength and favor upon those wrongfully detained for their faithfulness to you. Please give them the intrinsic sense that even in their current confined state, they can make an impact right where they are. Let those suffering for your purposes inspire all of us to do whatever we can wherever your will takes us.

Amen and Ase'.

Reflection/Affirmation

We are not forgotten. God knows our names, where we are, and where we are going. Consider the letters of Dietrich Bonhoeffer while in the Flossenburg concentration camp[47] and the letter of Dr. Martin Luther King, Jr. from the Birmingham jail.[48]

---

[47] Dietrich Bonhoeffer, *Letters and Papers from Prison*, ed. Eberhard Bethge (New York: Touchstone, 1997).

[48] Martin Luther King, Jr., "Letter from Birmingham Jail," April 16, 1963, in *Why We Can't Wait* (New York: Signet, 1964).

Day 34 (Saturday)

Death

By Bishop Sharma D. Lewis Logan

Scripture:

Mark 10:32-34 (NIV)

They were on their way up to Jerusalem, with Jesus leading the way, and the disciples were astonished, while those who followed were afraid. Again he took the Twelve aside and told them what was going to happen to him. "We are going up to Jerusalem," he said, "and the Son of Man will be delivered over to the chief priests and the teachers of the law. They will condemn him to death and will hand him over to the Gentiles, who will mock him and spit on him, flog him and kill him. Three days later he will rise."

Death is imminent. We will all face the reality of death and dying. But how would you react if your leader were able to predict their own death? How would you feel if you witnessed this leader raise the dead, heal the blind, walk on water, and describe the events of his own death? Unnerving to say the least!

In today's text, Jesus predicts his death for the third time as he travels with his disciples to Jerusalem. Jesus shares with the disciples what will happen to him once they reach the city. He describes in detail, "The Son of Man will be delivered over to the chief priests and teachers of the law. They will condemn him to death and will hand him over to the Gentiles, who will mock him and spit on him, flog him and kill him. Three days later he will rise" (Mark 10:33-34, NIV).

As Jesus describes his fate, he assures them that in three days, he will be resurrected. However, the disciples are shocked, while those who followed are frightened by the detailed account of his death. The disciples should not have been surprised by his prediction because this was their third discussion about his death and resurrection. Could it be that because Jesus spoke in parables, they thought this was another parable?

As we examine the text, Jesus' death was prophesied throughout the Bible in the Old and New Testaments—Psalm 22, Isaiah 52:13, Matthew 1:21, and Mark 8:31. Jesus was not surprised by his life circumstances; he embraced his death and resurrection. Paul writes in Philippians 2:8-9 (NIV), "And being found in appearance as a man, he humbled himself by becoming obedient to death—even death on a cross!" Titus 2:14 (NIV) says, "Who gave himself for us to redeem us from all wickedness and to purify for himself a people that are his very own, eager to do what is good." Scholars believe this sacrificial giving is a core tenet of the Christian faith, symbolizing God's immense grace.

Jesus' death gives us a new life. He died to reconcile humanity with God and provided us with everlasting life. As recorded in John 3:16 (NIV), "For God so loved the world that he gave his one and only Son, that whoever believes in him shall not perish but have eternal life." The Bible tells us in John 14:1-3 (NIV), "Do not let your hearts be troubled. You believe in God; believe also in me. My Father's house has many rooms; if that were not so, would I have told you that I am going there to prepare a place for you? And if I go and prepare a place for you, I will come back and take you to be with me that you also may be where I am." Isn't it reassuring to know that we have an eternal home with God?

Prayer

O Lord, let me live a life of righteousness to reap the eternal reward.

Amen.

Reflection

The disciples traveled and ministered with Jesus for three years. But did they understand the significance of the resurrection? Explain.

Day 35 (Monday)

Preparation Meets Opportunity

By Dr. Lewis E. Logan, II

Scripture:

Isaiah 42:1-9 (NLT)

"Look at my servant, whom I strengthen. He is my chosen one, who pleases me.
I have put my Spirit upon him. He will bring justice to the nations.
He will not shout or raise his voice in public.
He will not crush the weakest reed or put out a flickering candle. He will bring justice to all who have been wronged.
He will not falter or lose heart until justice prevails throughout the earth. Even distant lands beyond the sea will wait for his instruction."
God, the Lord, created the heavens and stretched them out. He created the earth and everything in it.
He gives breath to everyone, life to everyone who walks the earth.
And it is he who says, "I, the Lord, have called you to demonstrate my righteousness. I will take you by the hand and guard you, and I will give you to my people, Israel, as a symbol of my covenant with them.
And you will be a light to guide the nations.
You will open the eyes of the blind.
You will free the captives from prison, releasing those who sit in dark dungeons.

> *"I am the Lord; that is my name! I will not give my glory to anyone else, nor share my praise with carved idols. Everything I prophesied has come true, and now I will prophesy again.*
> *I will tell you the future before it happens."*

Historical Context

Isaiah 42:1-9 unfolds against the backdrop of the Assyrian and Babylonian empires. In such a challenging era, the community finds ways to cultivate ultimate hope, even as suffering weaves through their reality.

Hope and Suffering

Suffering becomes the setting in which restoration is imagined. The life and witness of the suffering servant "mirrors" the community's experience and reflects the enduring covenant of promised presence and restoration. Conflict is often present, but it is within this tension that hope is preserved.

Poetic Voice and Prophetic Perspective

Isaiah's words are part of a collection of poems crafted by a community of faith. These poetic compilations, preserved by the tradition of eighth-century prophets like Isaiah, provide a prophetic perspective and offer a portrait of Israel as the suffering servant. Familiar lines—such as "he was bruised for our transgressions; wounded for our iniquities"—emerge from this compilation, echoing throughout prophetic pronouncements.

Opportunity Amid Exile

Even in the hopelessness of exile, the suffering servant reveals opportunity. Throughout Christian church history, these moments of suffering give rise to meaning and collective agency. The presence of God in suffering becomes the means by which we face adversity, while fostering courage and intentionality.

Restoration and Messianic Hope

Restoration follows a season of suffering—just as Israel endured times of exile, turmoil, and oppression, both nationally and personally. The hope for a Messianic deliverer is ever-present, especially when daunting challenges arise.

Enduring Motif

The poetry of Isaiah becomes our poetry, offering connection, meaning, and motif. To suffer as a servant of God is not only requisite but also expected and expressed as what it means to be "known." This enduring message remains vital for communities navigating hardship, embracing hope, and embodying struggles for re-imagined realities.

Prayer

Lord, I'm grateful that your assigned suffering seasons are continually shaping me to serve you faithfully to make a relevant impact in this present age.

Amen and Ase'.

Reflection/Affirmation

Using inclusive language, read aloud Isaiah 42:1-7 and listen to your calling to serve the present age.

Day 36 (Tuesday)

Aged and In Trouble

By Bishop Sharma D. Lewis Logan

Scripture:

Psalm 71:1-14 (NLT)

O Lord, I have come to you for protection; don't let me be disgraced.
Save me and rescue me, for you do what is right.
Turn your ear to listen to me, and set me free.
Be my rock of safety where I can always hide.
Give the order to save me, for you are my rock and my fortress.
My God, rescue me from the power of the wicked, from the clutches of cruel oppressors.
O Lord, you alone are my hope. I've trusted you, O Lord, from childhood.
Yes, you have been with me from birth; from my mother's womb you have cared for me. No wonder I am always praising you!
My life is an example to many, because you have been my strength and protection.
That is why I can never stop praising you; I declare your glory all day long.
And now, in my old age, don't set me aside. Don't abandon me when my strength is failing.
For my enemies are whispering against me. They are plotting together to kill me.

They say, "God has abandoned him. Let's go and get him, for no one will help him now."

O God, don't stay away. My God, please hurry to help me.

Bring disgrace and destruction on my accusers. Humiliate and shame those who want to harm me.

But I will keep on hoping for your help; I will praise you more and more.

When I was growing up, my mother would often say, "When you are older, you will understand." Now that I'm older, I understand what my mother was trying to articulate. There is something about aging, wisdom, and experiences.

According to scholars, Psalm 71 was authored by a mature, anonymous person who was in trouble but confident that God would answer his prayers, based on two truths: God was his help and hope.

Psalm 71 is classified as a lament and has the following attributes:

- The psalmist always addresses God.
- The psalmist states the complaint.
- The psalmist articulates trust in God.
- The psalmist asks God for help in this particular situation.
- The psalmist expresses confidence in God's help.

The psalm is divided into three parts: each concluding on a note of praise—verses 1-8, 9-16, and 17-24. Verses 1-8 describe the psalm as a cry for help and a testimony of confidence. The first section of Psalm 71 begins, "In you, Lord, I have taken refuge; let me never be put to shame" (verse 1) and concludes with, "I have become a sign to many; you are my strong refuge. My mouth is filled with your praise, declaring your splendor all day long" (verses 7-8). In these verses, the mature psalmist expresses how God has been his constant help and protection since his youth.

Verses 9-16 describe the psalmist's prayer of regret. This section begins, "Do not cast me away when I am old; do not forsake me when my strength is gone. For my enemies speak against me, those who wait to kill me conspire together" (verses 9-10) and concludes, "My mouth will tell of your righteous deeds, of your saving acts all day long—though I know not how to relate them all. I will come and proclaim your mighty acts, Sovereign Lord; I will proclaim your righteous deeds, yours alone" (verses 15-16). In these verses, the mature psalmist expresses how committed he is to God in the midst of trouble.

Verses 17-24 describe the psalmist's prayer of praise. This third section begins, "Since my youth, God, you have taught me and to this day I declare your marvelous deeds" (verse 17) and concludes, "My tongue will tell of your righteous acts all day long" (verse 24). In these verses, the mature psalmist expresses praise to God with instruments, lips, and tongue.

Prayer

O Lord, let me serve you to the end of my life.

Amen.

Reflection

How do you anticipate serving God when you are a seasoned saint?

Day 37 (Betrayal Wednesday)

Inside Job

By Dr. Lewis E. Logan, II

Scripture:

John 18:1-19:42 (NLT)

After saying these things, Jesus crossed the Kidron Valley with his disciples and entered a grove of olive trees. Judas, the betrayer, knew this place, because Jesus had often gone there with his disciples. The leading priests and Pharisees had given Judas a contingent of Roman soldiers and Temple guards to accompany him. Now with blazing torches, lanterns, and weapons, they arrived at the olive grove.

Jesus fully realized all that was going to happen to him, so he stepped forward to meet them. "Who are you looking for?" he asked.

"Jesus the Nazarene," they replied.

"I am he," Jesus said. (Judas, who betrayed him, was standing with them.) As Jesus said "I am he," they all drew back and fell to the ground! 7 Once more he asked them, "Who are you looking for?"

And again they replied, "Jesus the Nazarene."

"I told you that I am he," Jesus said. "And since I am the one you want, let these others go." He did this to fulfill his own statement: "I did not lose a single one of those you have given me."

Then Simon Peter drew a sword and slashed off the right ear of Malchus, the high priest's slave. 11 But Jesus said to Peter, "Put your sword back into its sheath. Shall I not drink from the cup of suffering the Father has given me?"

So the soldiers, their commanding officer, and the Temple guards arrested Jesus and tied him up. First they took him to Annas, since he was the father-in-law of Caiaphas, the high priest at that time. Caiaphas was the one who had told the other Jewish leaders, "It's better that one man should die for the people."

Simon Peter followed Jesus, as did another of the disciples. That other disciple was acquainted with the high priest, so he was allowed to enter the high priest's courtyard with Jesus. Peter had to stay outside the gate. Then the disciple who knew the high priest spoke to the woman watching at the gate, and she let Peter in. The woman asked Peter, "You're not one of that man's disciples, are you?"

"No," he said, "I am not."

Because it was cold, the household servants and the guards had made a charcoal fire. They stood around it, warming themselves, and Peter stood with them, warming himself.

Inside, the high priest began asking Jesus about his followers and what he had been teaching them.

Then Andrew brought Simon to meet Jesus. Looking intently at Simon, Jesus said, "Your name is Simon, son of John— but you will be called Cephas" (which means "Peter)

The Significance of Spy Wednesday

Understanding the Day

This Wednesday of Holy Week bears many names: Betrayal Wednesday, Double Agent Wednesday, Spy Wednesday. Each label points to a central, sobering theme: betrayal, especially when it arises from someone close to us. The pain that comes from those nearest to our hearts is often the deepest, resonating with the psalmist's lament that it would hurt less if the wound came from a stranger, but it came instead from a companion in the assembly.

It is not an enemy who taunts me— I could bear that. It is not my foes who so arrogantly insult me— I could have hidden from them.

Instead, it is you—my equal, my companion and close friend.

What good fellowship we once enjoyed as we walked together to the house of God.

Psalm 55:12-15

The Pain of an Inside Job

Betrayal by someone we trust is uniquely challenging to overcome. The phrase "inside job" takes on new meaning here—for the harm is not just external; it does damage deep within. Jesus understood this pain intimately. He faced betrayal by one of his own, illustrating that greatness and purpose often walk hand in hand with disappointment and the wounds of broken trust. No one who has experienced betrayal, especially from someone close, can deny the profound impact it leaves on the spirit.

Judas and Historical Context

The very name "Iscariot" may hint at a link to the Sicarii, a group of radical assassins fiercely opposed to Roman rule—even to the point of targeting those within their own community who were seen as complicit with the oppressors. Judas, influenced by such zeal, may have believed he was helping to bring about a revolutionary change, hoping to force Jesus into a moment of divine intervention against the Roman Empire.

Betrayal with Purpose

Yet, the Gospel testifies that Jesus knowingly chose Judas, aware of his intentions and weaknesses. This is not to excuse the betrayal but to recognize that sometimes, even painful events have a place within a greater purpose. The journey through the wilderness of betrayal may be Spirit-led, reminding us that the Holy Spirit remains present, strengthening and fortifying us to endure and grow through even the most broken of relationships.

Enduring the Brokenness

Ultimately, the "inside job" of betrayal becomes an opportunity for the Spirit to work within us. The Holy Spirit fortifies us, enabling us to endure heartbreak and loss while discovering hope and resilience on the other side.

Prayer

Sometimes it's me, Lord. I confess that I'm your betrayer. Sometimes I betray you and what you intended for the life you imagined for me. Please forgive me for my twisted idolatry of forcing you into my image instead of reflecting your image in me. I lift before you my expectations, time frames, agendas, comparisons, frustrations, disappointments, and yes, my brokenness, as an offering of ultimate trust in you. Thank you, Lord, for making all things new, and I will follow you forward!

Amen and Ase'.

Reflection/Affirmation

My struggle with the Judas in me is an essential process of becoming more like the Jesus who is greater in me.

Day 38 (Maundy Thursday)

L-O-V-E

By Bishop Sharma D. Lewis Logan

Scripture:

John 13:31-35 (NIV)

When he was gone, Jesus said, "Now the Son of Man is glorified and God is glorified in him. If God is glorified in him,[a] God will glorify the Son in himself, and will glorify him at once.

"My children, I will be with you only a little longer. You will look for me, and just as I told the Jews, so I tell you now: Where I am going, you cannot come.

"A new command I give you: Love one another. As I have loved you, so you must love one another. By this everyone will know that you are my disciples, if you love one another."

The song "We are One in the Spirit" has always been a special song that I remember singing in church. However, the chorus, "And they'll know we are Christians by our love, by our love. Yes, they'll know we are Christians by our love,"[49] has always challenged me as a believer. Do we really show our love to the brother or

---

[49] Peter R. Scholtes, "They'll Know We Are Christians by Our Love," *The United Methodist Hymnal* (Nashville: United Methodist Publishing House, 1989), no. 2223.

sister who's different from us culturally, ethnically, or socioeconomically?

"Love" is described as an intense feeling of deep affection that has caused tears, heartbreak, joy, and happiness all at the same time. The Bible teaches us that love is the foundation of the Christian faith. It refers to the love of Jesus Christ for humanity, the love of Christians for Christ, and the love of Christians for others (John 15:9-17).

In John 13, we see Jesus washing the disciples' feet as an act of love and servanthood. Jesus reminds us in the Gospel of Matthew 20:28, "Just as the Son of Man did not come to be served, but to serve, and to give his life as a ransom for many." He identifies his betrayer, followed by the new commandment mandate. What is so powerful in this text is that Jesus loved them even though he knew that one would betray him, another would deny him, and all would temporarily abandon him.

In John 13:31-32, Jesus is revealed as the divine Son of God and Savior of the world by his death and resurrection. Five times in the conversation, Jesus uses the word "glory." According to *Nelson's Bible Dictionary*, "glory" represents the fullness of God's being, including God's goodness, faithfulness, power, holiness, and love.[50]

In John 13:34 (NIV), the text states, "A new command I give you: Love one another. As I have loved you, so you

---

[50] *Nelson's New Illustrated Bible Dictionary*, s.v. "Glory."

must love one another." This statement is reemphasized as the basis of the Jewish tradition as found in Leviticus 19:18 (NIV), "But love your neighbor as yourself." It is a theme cited repeatedly throughout the Old Testament.

Christ reminds us in John 13:35 that the disciples were commanded to love one another with the same kind of love that they had experienced from Jesus. This would be one of the ways they would be known and identified as his disciples.

Loving one another is the vital recipe in living for Christ and advancing the Kingdom. Love is a response, a way of living that is made possible by God's grace through the working of the Holy Spirit. As we learn to love others, it proves our spiritual maturity and our relationship to God. We must come to recognize that the love of God has no boundaries with regard to race, creed, sexual orientation, or color.

Loving one another is recognized as a reason for salvation and the knowledge of God found in 1 John 4:7-8 (NIV), "Let us love one another, for love comes from God. Everyone who loves has been born of God and knows God. Whoever does not love does not know God, because God is love." Knowing God, as revealed in 1 John 4:7, is an intimate and experiential knowledge of God.

In the Christian community, this day is referred to as Maundy Thursday, Holy Thursday, or Great Thursday. The word "Maundy" is derived from Latin and means a "new commandment." Services held on this evening typically include a reading from the Gospel account of the Last Supper, where Christ declares the bread and wine to be his body and blood. This day stresses Jesus' washing his disciples' feet at the beginning of the Last Supper. The washing of the feet is a traditional component of the celebration in many Christian churches, including the United Methodist, Presbyterian, and Roman Catholic churches.

Prayer

O Lord, let my actions be driven by my love.
Amen.

Reflection

In this stressful world, how do you show love in your actions?

Day 39 (Good Friday)

Bring it!

By Dr. Lewis E. Logan, II

Scripture:

Matthew 18:4-5 (NLT)

So anyone who becomes as humble as this little child is the greatest in the Kingdom of Heaven.

And anyone who welcomes a little child like this on my behalf is welcoming me.

Reflections on Courage

Scriptural Foundations

Several passages are suggested for reflection, each highlighting the fortitude and courage embodied by Jesus. The final Servant Song, the Hebrew reflection on the suffering of Jesus, Hebrews 4, and John 18 are all meaningful texts to consider. In John 18, Jesus steps forward at the time of betrayal, offering an inspiring example of courage.

Embracing the Spirit of Courage

Jesus knew what he would endure, yet he still stepped forward, guided by the Spirit of God. The same Spirit that led him through his season of trial led him to this defining moment. The Holy Spirit, present from the beginning, would also finish the work, demonstrating the completeness and faithfulness of God's presence.

The Power of the Holy Spirit and the Word

Other passages remind us of Jesus' use of Scripture during his temptation in the wilderness and throughout his ministry. From beginning to end, Jesus relied on both the same Spirit of God and the Word of God, available to every disciple. With such divine accompaniment, there is nothing that cannot be accomplished. Like Jesus, we are called to say, "Bring it."

Stepping Into Destiny

Jesus understood what was expected of him. He knew that destiny awaited and stepped into it courageously. This same courage is available to all disciples, empowering us to face any challenge and walk through any trial. We have all we need because God is our Jireh (provision).

Invitation to Reflect and Respond

You are invited to read these suggested passages and observe Jesus' courage. Draw on this courage as you face meaningful challenges and suffering. The call is to be fully present, amidst severe adversity, and to be available to confront evil. In the power of the Holy Spirit on this Good Friday, let us emulate Jesus' Spirit-led courage and declare together right now, "Bring it!"

Prayer

Lord Jesus, help me draw upon your courage as you stepped forward to embrace your destiny in the face of tremendous difficulty, opposition, and violence.

Amen and Ase'.

Reflection/Affirmation

I agree with you and the Word of God today, "If God be for me who can be against me!" (Romans 8:31, NKJV). The Lord is my strength, I will not fear. What can man do to me (Psalm 118:6 and Heb 13:6)? And, yes, I agree with rapper Bone Crusher, "I ain't never scared!"[51]

---

[51] Bone Crusher, "Never Scared," featuring Killer Mike and T.I., on AttenCHUN!, So So Def/Arista, 2003, CD and can be found at https://youtu.be/NeLtZ8K7EOM?si=gr_-wvGrgJl1Y6_8.

Day 40 (Holy Saturday)

What Will People Remember?

By Bishop Sharma D. Lewis Logan

Scripture:

John 19:38-42 (NIV)

Later, Joseph of Arimathea asked Pilate for the body of Jesus. Now Joseph was a disciple of Jesus, but secretly because he feared the Jewish leaders. With Pilate's permission, he came and took the body away. He was accompanied by Nicodemus, the man who earlier had visited Jesus at night. Nicodemus brought a mixture of myrrh and aloes, about seventy-five pounds. Taking Jesus' body, the two of them wrapped it, with the spices, in strips of linen. This was in accordance with Jewish burial customs. At the place where Jesus was crucified, there was a garden, and in the garden a new tomb, in which no one had ever been laid. Because it was the Jewish day of Preparation and since the tomb was nearby, they laid Jesus there.

When you are laid to rest, what will people remember about you? Will they remember you as the believer who led people to Christ? Will they remember you as the activist who fought for civil rights? Will they remember you as the devoted parent who wanted the best for their children?

Joseph of Arimathea and Nicodemus will be remembered as the two secret disciples who prepared

Jesus' body for burial. Joseph of Arimathea, "A member of the Council, a good and upright man, who had not consented to their decision and action" (Luke 23:50-51), asked Pilate's permission to bury Jesus' body in a rich man's borrowed tomb belonging to Joseph of Arimathea.

The text further reveals that Nicodemus, the man who visited Jesus earlier in the night, seeking truth about being "born again," "brought a mixture of myrrh and aloes, about seventy-five pounds" (John 19:39).

Pilate granted permission, and Jesus' body was taken down from the cross by Joseph of Arimathea and Nicodemus and "wrapped it, with the spices, in strips of linen" (John 19:14).

According to scholars, some think that John emphasized the new tomb so that after the resurrection, there could be no mistake in the identity of the burial place." Finally, according to Jewish customs, Jesus' burial was on the same day as his crucifixion (Deuteronomy 21:22-23). The burial of Jesus is described in the Gospels and fulfills a prophecy in Isaiah 53:9.

Prayer

O Lord, let my life be remembered. Amen.

Reflection

Reflect on your life. What would you want people to remember?

Group Study Guides

Group Study Guide 1
Ash Wednesday - Saturday

Theme
Beginning the journey of Lent by seeking authentic discipleship and repentance.

Crowdbreaker
Invite each participant to share one word that describes what they hope to experience this Lenten season.

Bible Study
Select one or two passages from this week to read as a group.

This week focuses on beginning the Lenten journey with humility and authenticity. Ash Wednesday reminds us that Lent is not about outward ritual alone but inward transformation. The scriptures call us to repentance, forgiveness, and renewal in preparation for the journey ahead.

Discussion Questions

- What does it mean to begin Lent with authenticity rather than empty ritual?
- How does understanding God's forgiveness shape how you forgive others?
- What spiritual practices will help you grow closer to God during Lent?

Wrap-Up
Lent begins with a call to return to God wholeheartedly, opening ourselves to transformation.

Closing Prayer
Lord, as we begin this Lenten journey, help us walk with humility, honesty, and grace. Amen.

Weekly Assignment
Reflect on what spiritual practices you will commit to during Lent. Write them down and pray over them daily.

Group Study Guide 2
Monday - Saturday
(Beginning the first Monday of Lent)

Theme

Exploring the depth of forgiveness and grace in our relationship with God and others.

Crowdbreaker

Share about a time when you experienced forgiveness, either given or received.

Bible Study

Select one or two passages from this week to read as a group.

This week emphasizes the necessity of forgiveness. Psalm 32 and related scriptures remind us that confession brings healing and freedom. God's forgiveness is limitless and calls us to forgive others in turn.

Discussion Questions

- Why is forgiveness essential to our spiritual health?
- What holds us back from confessing our sins to God?
- How can we extend grace to those who have hurt us?

Wrap-Up

Forgiveness is a key part of discipleship, freeing us to live in God's grace.

Closing Prayer

Gracious God, help us to forgive as you have forgiven us. Amen.

Weekly Assignment

Practice forgiveness this week by reaching out to someone who needs to hear words of grace from you.

Group Study Guide 3
Monday - Saturday
(Beginning the second Monday of Lent)

Theme

Learning to trust in God's help and to live with a childlike faith.

Crowdbreaker

Ask participants to share a childhood memory of trust and innocence.

Bible Study

Select one or two passages from this week to read as a group.

This week highlights childlike faith and trust in God. Just as Psalm 121 proclaims God as our helper, Jesus calls us to approach Him with humility and dependence, like a child.

Discussion Questions

- What does it mean to have a childlike faith as an adult?
- Where have you seen God's help in difficult times?
- How can we grow in trust and reliance on God this week?

Wrap-Up

Living with childlike faith means depending fully on God's love and guidance.

Closing Prayer

Lord, teach us to trust you completely, like children in the arms of a loving parent. Amen.

Weekly Assignment

Each day, write down one way you noticed God's presence and help in your life.

Group Study Guide 4
Monday - Saturday
(Beginning the third Monday of Lent)

Theme

Recognizing God's faithfulness and our call to worship and gratitude.

Crowdbreaker

Each participant shares their favorite worship song and why it is meaningful.

Bible Study

Select one or two passages from this week to read as a group.

Psalm 95 calls us to worship the Lord with joy and thanksgiving. Worship is both personal and communal, drawing us closer to God and each other. It reminds us of God's power, mercy, and love.

Discussion Questions

- How has worship shaped your faith journey?
- What distracts you from truly worshipping God?
- How can your daily life become an act of worship?

Wrap-Up

Worship reorients our hearts toward God and strengthens our community of faith.

Closing Prayer

O Lord, receive our praise and help us worship you with spirit and truth. Amen.

Weekly Assignment

Spend time each day in worship this week through prayer, song, or silent reflection.

Group Study Guide 5
Monday - Saturday

(Beginning the fourth Monday of Lent)

Theme

Embracing God's promise of renewal and the hope of new life.

Crowdbreaker

Have each participant share something in their life that God has renewed or restored.

Bible Study

Select one or two passages from this week to read as a group.

Ezekiel 36 reminds us that God brings renewal to His people. Just as God promises to give us a new heart and spirit, we are called to live into this hope as Easter approaches.

Discussion Questions

- Where do you need God's renewal in your life?
- How does hope in God's promises sustain you through difficult times?
- What does it mean to be a community shaped by renewal?

Wrap-Up

God is constantly at work bringing new life and transformation.

Closing Prayer

Lord, renew our hearts and fill us with hope as we walk toward Easter. Amen.

Weekly Assignment

Identify one area of your life where you need renewal and pray about it each day this week.

Group Study Guide 6
Monday - Saturday
(Beginning the fifth Monday of Lent)

Theme

Reflecting on Christ's sacrifice and the hope of resurrection.

Crowdbreaker

Invite participants to share what Easter means to them personally.

Bible Study

Select one or two passages from this week to read as a group.

As we enter Holy Week, we reflect on Christ's journey to the cross and the power of His resurrection. This final week draws us deeper into the mystery of God's love and the promise of eternal life.

Discussion Questions

- How does reflecting on Jesus' sacrifice impact your faith?
- What does the resurrection mean for your daily life?
- How can you share the message of Easter with others?

Wrap-Up

Christ's death and resurrection transform our lives and offer hope to the world.

Closing Prayer

Lord, prepare our hearts to celebrate the joy of resurrection. Amen.

Weekly Assignment

Spend time in prayer each day, focusing on gratitude for Jesus' sacrifice and the hope of Easter.

Final Week Study Guide
Holy Week: Monday - Holy Saturday

Theme

Walking with Christ through the events of Holy Week, reflecting on his suffering, death, and the anticipation of resurrection. This week invites us to enter deeply into the story of salvation and prepare our hearts for Easter.

Crowdbreaker

Invite participants to share one meaningful memory or tradition they have experienced during Holy Week or Easter in the past.

Bible Study

Holy Week takes us through the final days of Jesus' earthly ministry: his triumphal entry on Palm Sunday, the Last Supper, the agony in Gethsemane, his trial and crucifixion, and finally, the silence of Holy Saturday. Scripture readings such as Matthew 26-28, John 13-20, and Luke 22-24 guide us through these events. This is a week of deep reflection, confession, and hope as we await the joy of resurrection.

Discussion Questions

- Which part of the Holy Week story speaks to you most deeply this year?
- What spiritual practices can help you stay connected to God during this sacred week?
- How can you share the hope of Easter with others in a meaningful way?

Wrap-Up

Holy Week invites us to journey closely with Jesus, to sit in the grief of Good Friday and the waiting of Holy Saturday, so that we can fully experience the joy of Easter morning.

Closing Prayer

Lord, thank you for walking with us through this Lenten journey. As we remember your suffering and death, prepare our hearts to rejoice in the victory of your resurrection. May our lives reflect your grace and love in all we do. Amen.

www.ingramcontent.com/pod-product-compliance
Lightning Source LLC
Chambersburg PA
CBHW070613170426
43200CB00012B/2680